Greg Bruce was born on All Saints' Day and educated in Adelaide, South Australia. He attended Rose Park Primary School and Norwood High School. He acquired his medical degree from Adelaide University in 1970 and moved to New Zealand for his intern years immediately after graduation.

He remained in New Zealand to train in orthopaedic surgery and completed his last two years of training in the Royal National Orthopaedic Hospital in London, England. He then returned to an academic position in Sydney, Australia. Later, he moved into private practice.

He was recruited into the Royal Australian Air Force Specialist Reserve as an orthopaedic surgeon in 1988, and this led to the ten overseas deployments that are the subject of this book. He reached the rank of group captain and retired in 2013.

He received honours and awards during his service, including Membership of the Order of Australia.

This book is dedicated to my first wife, Glenys, who loved me so much, and I loved her more than I realised.

Equally dedicated to my sons, Matthew and Alexander; and my daughters-in-law, Melissa and Naomi; and my grandchildren, Archie, Freddie, Hugo, Cleo and Otto.

Equally dedicated to my dear wife, Gloria, who has provided loving support and tolerance when I have deployed.

Also dedicated to all of the comrades and colleagues with whom I have deployed, of all ranks, services, categories and musterings. There are too many to name in this book. I am grateful to all of them and I acknowledge all of them. I did not want to include some names and exclude others and so I have taken the easy option and put in no names. They all know who they are and I salute you all.

Greg Bruce

Greg Bruce

SAD JOYS ON DEPLOYMENT

AUSTIN MACAULEY PUBLISHERS™
LONDON • CAMBRIDGE • NEW YORK • SHARJAH

Copyright © Greg Bruce (2020)

The right of Greg Bruce to be identified as author of this work has been asserted by him in accordance with section 77 and 78 of the Copyright, Designs and Patents Act 1988.

All rights reserved. No part of this publication may be reproduced, stored in a retrieval system, or transmitted in any form or by any means, electronic, mechanical, photocopying, recording, or otherwise, without the prior permission of the publishers.

Any person who commits any unauthorised act in relation to this publication may be liable to criminal prosecution and civil claims for damages.

Austin Macauley is committed to publishing works of quality and integrity. In this spirit, we are proud to offer this book to our readers; however, the story, the experiences, and the words are the author's alone.

A CIP catalogue record for this title is available from the British Library.

ISBN 9781528905909 (Paperback)
ISBN 9781528905916 (Hardback)
ISBN 9781528958127 (ePub e-book)

www.austinmacauley.com

First Published (2020)
Austin Macauley Publishers Ltd
25 Canada Square
Canary Wharf
London
E14 5LQ

I would like to acknowledge and thank Susan Johnston for using her journalistic skills to advise on the text and suggest many changes for improvement. I have attempted to meet her high standards but have not always managed to do so. Any imperfections are my responsibility and not hers.

I would also like to thank Catherine Lewis, my sister, and Gloria Blonde, my wife, who both advised and suggested improvements.

Table of Contents

Chapter 1 — 13
First Blast Injury

Chapter 2 — 15
The Ten Deployments

Chapter 3 — 23
Victims

Chapter 4 — 26
Guns, Bombs and Injuries

Chapter 5 — 32
Disasters and the Familiar

Chapter 6 — 36
Surgeon's Comfort Zone

Chapter 7 — 39
Recruitment and Early Years

Chapter 8 — 43
Getting Ready

Chapter 9 — 46
Getting There

Chapter 10 — 51
The Military Base

Chapter 11   **57**
Base Security

Chapter 12   **61**
Personal Comfort and Health

Chapter 13   **69**
Workplace

Chapter 14   **82**
Military Hardware and Weapons

Chapter 15   **88**
Recreation on Base

Chapter 16   **93**
Exploring off Base

Chapter 17   **101**
Local Citizens

Chapter 18   **107**
Australian and Allied Defence Forces

Chapter 19   **115**
Hostile Forces

Chapter 20   **118**
UN and NGO

Chapter 21   **121**
Return Home

Chapter 22   **127**
Reflections

Chapter 23   **132**
A Reservist's Perspective of the Australian Defence Force

Epilogue 138

Appendix 141
  Daily Telegraph Articles Written in Balad, Iraq, in 2005

10 Jan, 2005 141
  Arrival

18 Feb, 2005 143
  ADF Med. Det. Balad

Mon, 31 Jan, 2005 145
  The Base

25 Jan, 2005 146
  The Hospital

19 Feb, 2005 148
  A Typical Day

5 Feb, 2005 150
  Mascal

30 Jan, 2005 151
  Election Day

6 Feb, 2005 152
  Noise

20 Feb, 2005 153
  The World Outside

Further Reading 172

Glossary of Terms/Abbreviations 173

Chapter 1
First Blast Injury

It was Monday, 12 June 1995, when the Australian Defence Force (ADF) surgical team landed in Kigali, the capital of Rwanda, in our scruffy C130 Hercules with UN markings but uncertain ownership. Our surgical team had arrived from Nairobi, Kenya, and comprised intensive care specialist, anaesthetist, general surgeon and myself as an orthopaedic surgeon. We were accompanied by two administrative army officers who had been sent to review the deployment, a task which was of the precise duration to qualify them for the Australian Active Service Medal (AASM). This coincidence was sufficiently noticeable for them to be dubbed as "gotta getta medal" by the troops who were enduring a six months deployment.

We were cleared through Kigali Airport that appeared modern but there were hundreds of bullet holes that had shattered windows, glass cases, floor tiles and lights.

We were driven from the airport on a confusing circuitous drive through dust, basic housing, rundown shops, some contrasting comfortable tree-lined streets and eventually to the ADF hospital to meet our Commanding Officer. He immediately introduced us to the departing surgical team for handover of current patients in the hospital, instruction on the facilities of the hospital and the type of work we could expect.

The handover did not even last five minutes. There was an emergency call from the resuscitation bay that a 12-year-old boy had stood on an anti-personnel mine and had severe injuries to both legs. Examining him revealed typical mine injuries with shredded skin, minced muscle, shattered bone, severed arteries and nerves. The eruption of the mine had forced filth and contamination deep into the layers of the flesh. A typical battlefield blast injury.

The departing and arriving general surgeons amputated the left leg below the knee and the departing orthopaedic surgeon and I amputated the right leg below the knee. The general surgeons removed an eye that had been penetrated by a fragment. A mangled little finger was amputated.

This was the first day that I had ever been deployed into a war zone as an orthopaedic surgeon with the Specialist Reserve of the Royal Australian Air Force (RAAF). It was my first experience of military battlefield surgery and it had happened within five minutes of arrival. How had I got into this situation and was I prepared for it?

The journey to Rwanda started in 1983 when I had a public hospital appointment in New South Wales, Australia. Political and ideological factors had made public hospitals unfriendly places for surgical specialists and so I was delighted to be offered a position as a civilian in RAAF 3 Hospital at Richmond Air Base, northwest of Sydney. I provided orthopaedic surgical services as a civilian for the next four years. In 1987, the Commanding Officer of the hospital invited me to join the RAAF Specialist Reserve and made it sound like an exclusive club. It sounded very appealing and so I said "yes".

The recruitment process took one year with lost forms and on-again/off-again interviews. The process ground on inexorably and, eventually in 1988, I was a member of my 'club' and began enjoying an easy military life.

Then followed a slow but relentless process of drawing me deeper and deeper into the role of a military orthopaedic surgeon. Some of the steps were basic officer training, provision of equipment, courses in aviation medicine, weapon training, military exercises within Australia, basic combat training and involvement in planning and administration of deployable surgical teams. The emphasis changed from my 'club' with the emphasis on mess dinners to a military orthopaedic surgeon who deployed ten times to war and disaster zones between 1995 and 2008 for a total period of about 14 months. Countries visited were Rwanda, Papua New Guinea, Bougainville, East Timor, the Solomon Islands, Iraq, Indonesia and Afghanistan.

Chapter 2
The Ten Deployments

This book summarises my ten deployments with the Australian Defence Force while I was a serving officer with the Royal Australian Air Force Specialist Reserve. It reflects on the experiences, similarities and differences of the various deployments. It will assist the reader's understanding if the deployments are briefly summarised.

My first deployment was to Kigali in Rwanda in 1995. It was my first active service overseas deployment and there was much that I needed to learn and much that I had learnt by the end of the deployment. One aspect was the discrepancy between the official task allocated by the Australian Commonwealth Government and the end result of the tasks achieved. The Government allocated the task to the Department of Defence of the Australian Public Service. The politicians and public servants instructed the senior officers of the Australian Defence Force (ADF) and they handed on the baton to the commanders within the area of operation in the country of the deployment. Changes happened as orders passed down the line.

The medical deployment to Rwanda occurred as a response to the terrible massacre of Tutsi by Hutu in late 1994, which was inevitably followed by reprisal massacres of Hutu by Tutsi. A United Nations Peacekeeping force was deployed to restore and maintain law and order until the country could get back onto its feet.

The medical deployment of the ADF consisted of full-time Australian Navy, Army and Air Force Medical Officers, Nursing Officers and Medics supported by ADF reservist specialists to provide surgical care. The deployed specialists were a general surgeon, orthopaedic surgeon, anaesthetist and intensive care specialist. Our official task was to provide medical support for the UN peacekeeping force called UNAMIR. In fact, there was 'mission creep' or 'flexibility of tasking' so that we spent a substantial period of time, effort and resources treating local Rwandan civilians. We also treated serving members of the triumphant Rwandan Patriotic Army (RPA) who were Tutsi and were currently in power. Treatment of RPA members by UN staff was not permitted but they had ways of sneaking in and we had ways of not noticing.

The other big lesson was the inadequacy and 'paper tiger' aspect of the UN, but more of that in a later chapter.

The deployment lasted for nine weeks. We trained in Sydney. We flew to Nairobi by civilian aircraft and then to Kigali on a UN-chartered C130 Hercules that was scarcely serviceable. This was my first experience of UN cost-cutting and quest for the cheapest option, regardless of any risk to personnel. Security guards at the trashed Kigali Airport were closely watching TV screens of luggage being X-rayed, the effect being spoilt because the screens were all blank. We travelled from the airport to accommodation by Land Rover along dusty red roads amongst tiny motorbikes that were carrying extended families with their luggage.

Our accommodation was in the UN hospital and was separate from UN HQ where all of the infantry were located. It was about a five-minute walk from the secure UN HQ and was situated next to the RPA barracks that had demonstrated animosity towards Australian soldiers. When we walked between hospital and HQ, we were always escorted by an Australian Army infantryman carrying a Minimi machine gun.

The accommodation and the UN hospital were in a devastated private hospital that had been resurrected sufficiently to provide operating theatres, an intensive care unit and patient wards. There were the usual Rwandan bullet holes, smashed windows and bloodstains on the floor. I had a room to myself with an en-suite toilet of sorts. The communal shower was usually cold but occasionally hot. The unpredictability of the hot water made it more frustrating than if it had simply been cold water for the entire stay.

Our mission was to provide medical support for a distressed country that was trying to recover from the horrendous massacre of Tutsi by Hutu. Tutsi had regained control of the country and were itching to wreak revenge. The UN had the unenviable task of maintaining peace. The ADF medical team was providing medical support for UN personnel and an Australian Army Infantry Company had been deployed to keep the medical team secure. Patients presented from all sources, UN military personnel, UN civilians, Non-Government Organisation (NGO) civilians, Rwanda Patriotic Army members, Rwandan VIPs and local civilians. The local health service had been devastated by the murder of health workers and the destruction of hospitals and clinics. The local public hospital was staffed by junior doctors, medical students and nurses. It was scarcely coping and so the ADF medical team frequently visited to help on the wards and in the operating theatre.

My second deployment was to Vanimo in Papua New Guinea for two weeks in urgent response to a tsunami that struck the northeast coast of the country in July 1998. This was one of the most satisfying and interesting of my deployments. The task was an urgent response to a humanitarian disaster and there was a great sense of achievement for the overall good of humanity, though it was in a relatively minor way. The deployment was reactive rather than planned and so there was an element of *ad hoc* planning and improvisation. There was less control from remote commanding officers and much more 'on the spot' decision-making. I arrived a few days after the main party and so missed the most interesting phase. However, I was still able to experience the 'charms' of a deployment such as 'dossing down' with stretchers and hoochies in a school change room with showers, innovative anaesthesia and desperate surgery in a tent, the gratitude and assistance of the local civilians, the altruistic assistance of the Catholic Church, hailing aircraft on runways as if they were taxis and then hoping that they were travelling in the right direction. We did a bit of good but I believe the engineers and environmental health officers did better with much less publicity.

My third deployment was to Bougainville in November 1998 as part of the medical support team for the ADF Peace Monitoring Group (PMG) in Loloho at the end of their civil war.

Bougainville is situated between Papua New Guinea (PNG) and the Solomon Islands in the South Pacific Ocean and was included in the Territory of New Guinea administered by Australia after World War I. It was then joined to the nation of PNG when it gained independence in 1975, even though there were geographical and ethnic differences. Bougainville has long sought independence from PNG, not least because it is the site of a major copper mine that was a source of considerable wealth while it was functioning. The end result was a civil war with PNG that has been described as the largest armed conflict in the South Pacific since World War II and inevitably resulted in the closure of the mine. Also messy were the complicated political and murderous battles between various factions in Bougainville with considerable involvement by the PNG Government that was trying to retain control of one of its major assets. Eventually there was a truce, Bougainville was given partial autonomy and long-term plans were made for a referendum on independence in 2019. There have been tentative plans to re-open the mine but it has not yet happened.

Bougainville is a perfect case study of the human species' remarkable ability to spoil paradise.

The civil war waged for nine years and Bougainville regressed to a tragically primitive society over those years. Prominent citizens who could contribute to the general welfare were murdered and infrastructure was destroyed. Schools were closed. We met twenty-four-year-olds who were returning to the school which they had left at the age of fourteen or fifteen. Medical services were non-existent. Casualties with severe injuries were dumped in the jungle to die and childbirth was Russian roulette. Our job in the medical team was to provide health services to the deployed PMG forces and also to provide some sort of health service to the local citizens using the hopelessly inadequate facilities and equipment that had survived. Training local health personnel was the biggest favour we could do for the country.

The PMG was deployed to the devastated port of Loloho where the copper from the mine had been partially processed and exported.

My fourth, fifth and sixth deployments were to Dili in East Timor. The task was primarily medical support for defence force personnel and civilians who had been sent to East Timor at the end of 1999 to assist the country with its difficult birth as an independent democracy following a violent and fiery separation from Indonesia. We also treated members of NGOs, civilian contractors, East Timorese with influence and anyone else who was dumped at the front gate.

We provided moral, material and practical support for the local public hospital, which was also supported by visiting teams from the International Committee of the Red Cross (ICRC). It was also supported by international civilian assistance, including a Norwegian transportable hospital that was on the grounds of the public hospital, but I do not believe it was ever unpacked. I never saw it in action. Inevitably, it would have run into problems of re-supply of the large amounts of disposable equipment required to keep a hospital running. The bricks and mortar were not the problem. The problem was the lack of skilled humans to do the work. Quality medical and nursing staff had disappeared either overseas or into the countryside.

The first East Timor deployment was under the command of the ADF legitimised by the umbrella of INTERFET (International Force in East Timor). INTERFET was a coalition of international defence forces that was raised and coordinated by the Australian Government with UN approval but not under direct UN command. Presumably, the Australian Government was reluctant to cede excessive power and command over ADF members to the UN in such a volatile environment. There are examples of UN decisions made remotely from head office being so timid or indifferent that there have been disastrous consequences for the troops on the spot.

I had my first Christmas on deployment in Dili in 1999 and saw in the new millennium one week later.

By the time of my second and third deployments in East Timor, the situation had stabilised sufficiently for the UN to be allowed control. We were under the command of a body identified as UNTAET (UN Transitional Administration in East Timor) and the Peace Monitoring Force was much more multinational. The hospital was now called UNMILHOSP (UN Military Hospital) and we were sharing the hospital with the Egyptian Army. RAAF had overall command and the CO was an excellent Wing Commander who juggled the international protocols successfully. The CO of the Egyptian contingent was more highly ranked, but fortunately he sidestepped major clashes by residing outside the hospital in comfortable circumstances that he regarded as more appropriate to his rank. He only visited the hospital occasionally, thus minimising fuss and bother.

Dili is the capital city of East Timor and it was interesting to observe the incremental improvement deployment by deployment. The showers progressed from camp-style cold water bags to demountable shower and toilet blocks with hot and cold running water. The personal living space progressed from a tiny room for four people, with only a stretcher available for storage of personal items and sleeping, to a large tent the second time and then to a personal room in a demountable hut on the third visit. The hospital facilities and equipment also improved but, conversely, the workload decreased as the situation became more peaceful and the local hospital increased its level of function.

My seventh deployment was to Honiara in the Solomon Islands in December 2003 and was based at the famous Henderson Airport. Henderson Air Field was the impetus for the titanic struggle between Japan and the USA during the Battle of Guadalcanal in World War II. It was the pivotal battle of the South Pacific.

The Solomon Islands are east of Australia and north of New Zealand. The independent nation is an amalgam of islands each populated by islanders with subtle cultural and social differences. Inevitably, when humans are put into this type of situation, there will be dysfunctional interaction between them and sometimes this will degenerate into hostilities. The dispute between the Malaita Eagle Force and the seat of power in Honiara, Guadalcanal, led to civil war which only ended after intervention from neighbours such as Australia and New Zealand. A peace monitoring force called the Regional Assistance Mission to Solomon Islands (RAMSI) was deployed with the blessing of the UN. The ADF medical team's task was health support for the deployed forces which included defence force members and members of the Australian Federal Police (AFP). The local health system was functioning well and did not need any help. Nonetheless, we visited and observed for mutual information and collegiality. Otherwise, the workload was light and there was considerable spare time for interesting activities such as Guadalcanal battlefield tours, flights to outlying islands hanging out the back of a RAAF Caribou and sitting on the beach while watching crocodiles swimming past. I spent my second deployed Christmas in Honiara. The Solomon Islands was the quietest of my deployments but enjoyable and interesting nonetheless.

The next deployment to Iraq was my eighth and was in complete contrast to the Honiara deployment. It was the longest, most confronting, most stressful, most demanding and most interesting of all. If I was given the choice of only doing one of my deployments, this would be the one. I deployed in late 2004 after the USA had declared "Mission Accomplished" in Iraq but was still having problems establishing any type of control in the country, let alone normal civilised law and order. Insurgency, terrorism, suicide bombings, roadside bombs, kidnappings for ransom, beheadings, random murder, sabotage and combat between many hostile forces were the order of the day. The coalition forces led by the USA and NATO were not welcomed with open arms, to say the least, and enmity between factions, regions, Muslim sects and neighbouring countries was also added to the mix. The end result was a constant stream of a variety of casualties from many sources.

The base was at Balad and was previously the main training academy for the Iraqi Air Force. It had been smashed by the US and coalition forces before the fall of Saddam Hussein, the former dictator of Iraq, and was littered with the wrecks of aircraft, tanks and concrete bunkers shaped like upside-down saucers. The aircraft were MIG-29 and MIG-21 and the tanks were T-72, all from Russia. The base had been taken over by the US defence force and put under USAF command. It was 25 square miles in size and occupied by tens of thousands of US and coalition forces and civilians. It had many roles such as reception and dispatch of huge amounts of equipment and war materiel by air and monster sized road convoys, tactical posting of F16 Fighting Falcon fighters, provision of local security and, relevant to myself, the location of one of the two major military US defence force hospitals in the Middle East.

The hospital provided emergency medicine, trauma surgery, intensive care and aero-medical evacuation for combat casualties. Occasional civilian style of trauma, such as sports injuries or work accidents, was a distracting side issue.

There were two main sources of patients. The surrounding countryside was infested with insurgents who were targeting the occupying coalition forces and any local civilians who were perceived as not supporting the insurgency. Suicide bombings and high-velocity gunshot wounds were common, such as a suicide bomber who exploded at the front gate of the base and killed a large number of local civilians who were reporting to work in the hope of improving their shattered lives. The hospital was also the staging facility for aeromedical evacuation of coalition casualties. The huge majority of these were US defence force personnel, almost exclusively US Army and US Marines. Those who were wounded up-country had initial wound surgery in a forward surgical facility and then were air transported to Balad for air transfer to a US military hospital in Landstuhl, Germany, and then on to the USA for definitive reconstruction surgery and rehabilitation. They usually arrived in Balad in the middle of the night and each casualty was taken to the operating theatre and the initial wound surgery was repeated to prevent increasing infection and reduce the risk of complications such as gas gangrene during their long trip home. We also had a steady flow of US casualties from the immediate surrounds of the base where contacts with insurgents were still a regular event.

I was part of a RAAF medical team that was embedded into the USAF hospital to complement and enhance their medical services. We were under US control relevant to medical aspects but remained under ADF military command so that we could avoid any misunderstandings that may have occurred under US military command. The deployment lasted a total of three months in the country and a further month in pre-deployment training and post-deployment extraction and debriefing. It was four months out of my civilian professional life and it took a while to get back to speed on my return.

Our relationship with the USAF medical team was very good as demonstrated by this letter. It was written by a USAF Colonel Surgeon in Iraq to his father, explaining the character of the Aussie health professionals with whom he was working within the Middle East Area of Operations (MEAO).

'The Aussies are unique. In the first place, not only did they have to volunteer to come here to Balad, but they also have to compete to get a slot. All of the Aussies are dedicated, motivated and extremely good at what they do. They are the best of the best, and I have to scramble to keep up with them clinically. The other thing they bring to the fight is that most of them are veterans of East Timor and Bougainville, and they have seen most of what comes through the door many times before. We would be hard pressed to run the hospital without them. As a group, they seem to be very practical people, and I think they are the way people used to be on the American Frontier. They are self-reliant, confident, and they never do anything halfway. If they are going to do it, they do it right. I run into them frequently when walking through the hall because they always want to pass on the right, which I think, comes from driving on the left side of the road. They tend to be direct in speech and action. This morning during the rounds there was a concern for a patient who had sustained an IED blast, and the Australians were busy sorting it out in a professional manner.'

The hospital was large and had many specialists. There were three or four orthopaedic surgeons, five or six general surgeons with subspecialties such as thoracic and vascular, neurosurgeon, eye surgeon and ear, nose, and throat surgeon. It also had the ancillaries of a major trauma hospital such as laboratory, X-ray, CT scans, physiotherapy and intensive care with ventilators for assisted breathing.

The base was a small stronghold of the USA in hostile surroundings. No one ventured off base unless they were heavily armed, wearing armour and in company with a significant force of comrades in an appropriate armoured vehicle. The less friendly locals regularly fired mortar bombs and rockets onto the base, on average about three to four times each day. The base commanders proudly described Balad as "the most attacked base in Iraq".

The ninth deployment was brief but dramatic. It was in response to the second terrorist bombing in Bali, Indonesia, that occurred on 1 October 2005. Three explosions occurred around 7 pm. Twenty people were killed, four of them Australian, and over hundred were injured, 19 of them Australian. I was part of the RAAF aeromedical evacuation (AME) team that had been expanded to a surgical capability. In other words, the team included two surgeons and two anaesthetists in addition to the usual intensivist and AME qualified RAAF Medical Officer and also carried extra equipment. Our task was immediate care and evacuation of the injured Australians. At the time of the first Bali bombing in 2002, there had been problems transporting the injured to the airport from local hospitals or directly from the site of the bombings. On this occasion, an advance party had been sent to facilitate intelligence of the situation and to expedite the transport of casualties to the airport. They were closely followed by the first AME C-130 Hercules and the RAAF personnel assisted with casualty transfer. I was on the second C-130 and found most of the casualties were on stretchers under shelter at the airport, already assessed and awaiting evacuation. We contributed to their treatment and stabilisation for air evacuation and then supervised them boarding the two aircraft that had brought the medical teams. The aircraft left and we remained in Bali while we waited for arrangements to be made for our transport home. This took a few days, which was awkward, as none of us had taken any personal gear because of weight restrictions and the expectation that we would be returning home immediately with the casualties. We were isolated in a foreign country, dressed in ADF uniforms and fulfilling no particular purpose. We were transferred to a local multi-starred hotel and stayed out of sight for two or three days until we flew back on a civilian QANTAS flight.

The tenth deployment in 2008 saw a return to the Middle East as the orthopaedic surgeon component of an ADF Medical Task Force. We were deployed to provide surgical, anaesthetic and intensive care support for a major military hospital owned and commanded by the defence force of the Netherlands. It was located at a NATO airbase at Tarin Kowt in Oruzgan province of Afghanistan.

There were similarities and differences of the deployment to Balad in Iraq. This deployment was less busy, but almost as stressful because our team was the only surgical team in the area looking after NATO personnel. There was only one anaesthetist, one general surgeon and one orthopaedic surgeon and so we were on call and available twenty-four hours a day, seven days a week and there was no collegial support from colleagues. The workload was less busy than in Balad. There was not the same element of mass casualties and the types of injury were not as severe. This was a reflection of the exceptionally hazardous, anarchic and violent situation in Iraq in 2004. We were accommodated in secure armour-plated shelters and the hospital was similarly protected. It had been purchased and developed specifically for the deployment by the Netherlands. The deployment lasted six weeks in Tarin Kowt and there were also the added weeks of pre-deployment training and post-deployment de-briefing. The work was steady rather than busy and was a mixture of NATO combat casualties and local civilians who had been significantly harmed by one of their countrymen. A contrast with Iraq was that there were more gunshot and knife injuries and fewer suicide bombings.

These were the ten deployments that provided the experience for this book. There were similarities and contrasts in the deployments. My ability to cope with the deployments improved as I gained experience but, conversely, lessons learnt from one deployment were not necessarily applicable for the next. This was relevant to the management of surgical cases such as selection of a patient for surgery and then performing an operation appropriate to local conditions. Equally, some lessons were universally applicable for all deployments and there were problems if they were disregarded. Specific examples of this are the personal relationships with comrades and colleagues such as higher-ranking officers, 'other ranks', defence personnel from other countries and local civilians. Disregarding the written and unwritten rules causes problems and there were examples of this in each of the deployments.

The following chapters in this book document the comparisons and contrast the many facets of the deployments.

Chapter 3
Victims

The location and task of each deployment were different, thus the patients and casualties varied on each deployment.

In Rwanda, the primary task of the surgical team was to provide medical support for the deployed UN forces from countries such as Australia, India, Uganda and the United Kingdom. The servicemen and women were in a UN Peace Monitoring role and not actively involved in hot military action. The UN military were young, fit and actively participating in sport and fitness training but were not in combat on the battlefield. Orthopaedic problems were more characteristic of the injuries that occur in young people training and competing in a sport. Ligament sprains and simple fractures were the order of the day for UN personnel.

Care for Rwandan civilians was not our prime task but we frequently treated them, which was personally satisfying for the UN medical team but was only scratching the surface of the medical deficiencies of the country. It was the continuing question as to whether 'first world' surgical visitors to a 'third world' country are pandering to their own self-satisfaction more than providing a tangible benefit to the recipient third-world citizens.

The injuries, diseases and treatment of Rwandan civilians were different from those of the deployed UN personnel. Some Rwandans were treated after being transferred from the local hospital. Some were treated for conditions or injuries that had occurred a long time previously, such as old gunshot wounds from the civil war over the previous 12 months. Some had been injured in the usual accidents that occur everywhere in the world. Falls, road accidents, work injuries and misfortune at home will always happen and provide a constant need for an orthopaedic surgeon, no matter how unique the location or civil disruption. Others had battlefield-type blast injuries from the numerous mines lying around haphazardly. Many anti-personnel mines had been scattered throughout populated areas during the civil war and there was no clear record of their location. Walking through fields and areas of vegetation was always a danger, particularly after heavy rain which could wash these light, plastic menaces into a different place. A well-trodden path may be safe one day but become a threat to life or limb after heavy rain. Gunshot wounds and machete wounds were commonplace following private disputes or arbitrary punishments dispensed by those in power.

In Iraq and Afghanistan, the coalition forces were on active service and were regularly engaged in military combat. Deadly attacks on convoys and patrolling troops were common and bombs, booby-traps, mines, rocket-propelled grenades (RPG) and small arms fire were the favoured weapons. Battlefield injuries were common and were rapidly evacuated to the transportable field hospitals, preferably within an hour or less. Broken and bleeding casualties arrived soon after their injury and could deteriorate and perish rapidly unless expertly treated.

The military bases were large, densely populated and crammed with heavy, complex weapons, military vehicles and other paraphernalia that were waiting to hurt the unwary. Industrial, traffic and sports injuries contributed to the orthopaedic workload. Local civilians were not exempt from bombs and blasts and made up about half of the clientele. They presented additional problems of continuity of treatment. Coalition members were evacuated by air within forty-eight hours but local civilians did not have that luxury.

Military hospitals focus on immediate casualty care followed by rapid evacuation and are not equipped or staffed for the reconstruction and rehabilitation of long care patients. This was a problem that was not resolved during my stay in-country and could only be resolved when the local health service got back online and resumed care for their local civilians. It is a mistake for an occupying military force to become the *de facto* health service for a country while waiting for the resumption of normal health services. Military health services are better equipped and staffed compared to the services provided by a failing country and can provide such a good service that there is no stimulus for the local service to return to normal.

Casualties treated during humanitarian assistance following a natural disaster, such as the tsunami in north-west Papua New Guinea, contrast dramatically with battlefield casualties following military combat.

Military medical facilities are put in place in anticipation of casualties during military action and are organised to evacuate the casualties very rapidly so that they arrive very soon after their injury. Statistics show a broad trend of three peaks of fatalities when there are mass casualties. Some are killed instantly. Some have life-threatening wounds and perish within the first hour if not skilfully treated within that first hour. Hence the term 'golden hour' when action is vital to save lives. Some survive for two or three weeks and then die of complications such as infection or failure of vital body systems, particularly the heart, lungs or kidneys. Top quality military health services can successfully treat the second two categories following combat because battlefield casualties are immediately transported for treatment and usually arrive within the hour.

Victims of natural disasters are not so blessed. The PNG Tsunami was typical. It was known that there had been an earth tremor offshore from PNG and a tsunami was predicted but there was no communication from the site and no information available. An RAAF C130 Hercules overflew the location within 12 hours and confirmed the disaster. Diplomatic communication between the PNG and Australian Governments commenced and assistance was planned and deployed. All of this takes time and ADF military health facilities were on the ground after 48 hours, which was an outstanding and rapid achievement but, inevitably, it meant that the second category described above, those dependent on help in the 'golden hour', could not survive and had already perished. Humanitarian aid in this situation mainly consists of preventing fatal complications in the survivors and replacing the devastated local health facilities until it comes back online.

The big difference between military medical surgery and the surgery of humanitarian assistance is that the former gets casualties very quickly and treats potentially fatal injuries during the 'golden hour'. 'Triage' is the term for differentiating between salvageable and non-salvageable casualties. The term 'natural triage' is used in natural disasters because the delay in getting quality medical care into a disaster zone within the first 'golden hour' means that the victims at risk of the second peak of fatalities do not survive.

Chapter 4
Guns, Bombs and Injuries

Military surgery is so different from civilian surgery that surgeons need special training and instruction to qualify as a 'military surgeon'. This becomes apparent when civilian surgeons are required to operate in a military setting without training or previous experience, as can happen unpredictably. Civilians may be injured by military-style weapons during terrorist attacks in normally peaceful cities and are then treated in hospitals more accustomed to routine non-military injuries. This has occurred in Madrid, London and Paris. A country's citizens may be wounded during a terrorist attack while travelling overseas and then evacuated back home to the care of a civilian hospital with civilian staff. This happened with the Australian victims of the Bali bombings. Civilian surgeons can deploy with Non-Government Organisations and find themselves out of their comfort zone dealing with military injuries which they have never previously treated.

Even surgeons who are members of a defence force can be caught out. US defence force surgeons were primarily treating routine, non-combat types of diseases and injuries suffered by their defence force members and families prior to the huge US military deployments to the Middle East after the 9/11 World Trade Centre atrocities. Their military medical practice was a replica of civilian medical practice in the USA. The surgeons had to rapidly relearn the lessons from previous wars such as World War II, the Korean War and the Vietnam War. The rapid recognition of the problem, gathering of data, delineating principles and training specialists was a great achievement by the senior health officers in the US defence forces. Some of the changes in trauma management were trailblazing in the medical profession and have now found their way into civilian trauma medicine. Perhaps the only benefit of war is advance in science including medical science.

Why are injuries due to military weapons so different? Why do they need to be treated differently? How do military equipment and resources make a difference to the casualty that is delivered to the surgeon? Do civilians have different injuries from the sailors, soldiers and airmen of defence forces? These are questions all surgeons must ask themselves before treating battlefield casualties.

Military weapons are designed to damage human bodies and their military equipment. The projectiles travel at high speeds, they explode and they get hot. Homemade roadside bombs are as lethally damaging as the products of the weapon companies that research and manufacture ordnance commercially.

The high speeds of high-velocity gunshot wounds impact destructive kinetic energy on the human body. Bone does not simply break when it is struck by a high-velocity bullet, it shatters into many pieces. The surrounding structures such as skin, muscles, arteries, veins and nerves are smashed and become useless dead tissue. This dead soft tissue will become infected if left in the wound and the worst cases will get gas gangrene or tetanus. The projectiles carry contamination and there is further soiling of the wound when the casualty hits the ground. The wound becomes a polluted soup of bone fragments, dead soft tissue and dirt. Typical of a high-velocity gunshot wound is a small entrance wound followed by shattering of the bullet and tissue and then a large exit wound as it all blows out the other side of the limb or body. There is a lot of dirty dead tissue between the small entrance wound and the large exit wound.

The explosion of a mine, grenade or Improvised Explosive Device (IED or homemade bomb) causes a surge of high-pressure which turns normal tissue to a pulp. All organs are susceptible such as the brain, the lungs and heart, contents of the abdomen, contents of the pelvis and the structures of the limbs. Fragments of the exploding weapon and external debris such as stones and gravel are driven into the victim. There is immense damage to all parts of the body from the shockwave of the explosion and the flying fragments of shrapnel and stones. These are the typical injuries of mines, grenades, homemade bombs and artillery rounds.

Explosions are scorching hot and severe burns add to the awful injuries.

A high-velocity gunshot wound is usually a single devastating wound with only one body part or system damaged. Blast injuries cause multiple wounds to multiple body parts and multiple organ systems. There can be brain injury, lung injury, bowel injury and multiple fractures. Many different specialists may be required to work simultaneously to salvage the patient. This may be difficult when there is only one surgeon and one anaesthetist.

Defence forces expect their fighters to suffer wounds and so they deploy medical teams to treat casualties instantly. Casualty care is carried out on the battleground by combat medics and the victim is then transferred through tiers of increasing medical capability until they reach the level that matches their injury. Casualties who need surgery should reach a surgical team in less than one hour. Military surgeons are resuscitating and operating on casualties who are grievously injured but still alive. Be quite clear on this. These injuries are much more severe than occur in civilian life but the casualties reach high-quality surgical care and are taken into the operating theatre much earlier than occurs with civilian casualties in civilian hospitals.

Surgeons inexperienced in military surgery struggle with the severity of the casualties who are still haemorrhaging, suffocating, burning or brain dying. These injuries do not occur in civilian life and, even if they did, the civilian infrastructure does not have medics, helicopters and surgical teams in the immediate vicinity. In a civilian setting, most of these casualties would have died before the ambulance arrived, let alone reached the emergency department of a hospital. Yet a modern military hospital can achieve 98% survival rate of any living casualty who reaches their resuscitation bay. The speed of the retrieval system, the quality of the casualty facilities and the training of the medical personnel gives the combat casualty the greatest chance to survive.

Body armour has changed the pattern of injuries because it protects the vulnerable vital organs in the chest, abdomen and pelvis. Helmets protect the brain. The eyes, face and limbs are exposed. If body armour is not worn, bomb blasts injure unprotected parts of the body, such as the trunk, and the casualty can rapidly die from chest and abdominal injuries. Body armour protects these areas so that the casualty becomes one of the 98% who reach the resuscitation bay and is saved. However, the unprotected areas such as face and limbs are injured and so now there is a much higher percentage of facial fractures, penetrating eye injuries and limb injuries with mangled bone, muscle, nerve and blood vessels.

Civilian victims of bomb blasts are unlikely to be wearing body armour and helmets and so there is a higher fatality rate and a higher percentage of severe injuries to lungs, heart, liver, bowel and pelvic organs.

'Bomb' is too simple and emotive a description for the military and so the passion is removed by calling it an Improvised Explosive Device (IED), a term which has now been accepted in general communication and is on the verge of developing its own level of emotion.

A typical blast injury to a soldier occurred within days of my deployment to Iraq. An armoured Humvee with two soldier occupants ran over an IED. The driver was killed instantly and the passenger was admitted with devastating injuries to both lower limbs. One leg was amputated below the knee and the other was amputated above the knee. One arm was lacerated and fractured but was salvageable. He suffered a minor injury to one eye. Nonetheless, he did not suffer major head injury because he was wearing a helmet, the eye injury was minor because he was wearing eye protective goggles and he did not suffer major chest, abdominal or pelvic injuries because he was wearing body armour. He survived because there was no major organ damage. This is the pattern of the modern military casualty. There are major limb injuries and significant risk of eye and facial injury but major trunk injuries are less common. Body armour has made big changes to the pattern of military injuries and has increased the chances of survival for soldiers but has also increased the need for orthopaedic surgeons in combat zones.

This contrasts with a civilian who may be injured by a similar weapon but does not have the advantage of similar protective armour for head, face and body. The civilian will suffer similar injuries to the fully equipped soldier but with head, facial, abdominal and thoracic injuries added for good measure.

An illustrative case that I treated in Iraq was a 50 to 60-year-old woman who was admitted to our hospital. Fewer women than men civilians were admitted in Iraq, partly because men were more frequently in places of danger and partly because of the cultural concern of women being isolated in a western-style hospital staffed by a mixture of men and women. This woman's only crime was that her daughter was working as an interpreter with the coalition forces because no men remained with the family and she provided the sole source of income. There was a knock at the door and, when it was opened, a bomb was thrown and the woman suffered multiple injuries. She was flown to our hospital by US helicopter evacuation.

She suffered the blast impact of the bomb combined with the multiple projectiles contained in the device. She was concussed. A fragment penetrated one eye which necessitated surgical removal of the eye. She suffered fractures and lacerations to the bones and skin of her face sufficient to prevent her breathing through her nose and mouth. An artificial airway was inserted surgically through the windpipe in her neck and miniature plates and screws were used to fix the facial fractures. Fragments had penetrated her chest causing a lung to collapse. This was treated with a chest drain. Fragments had penetrated her abdomen and the bowel had been perforated. The abdomen was opened and severely damaged bowel was removed. The bowel was deviated through the wall of her abdomen until function returned. My role was confined to fractures of varying severity that had occurred in all four limbs with severe wounds to the overlying skin and muscles. Some of her limb injuries needed simple cleaning while some needed complex external fixation of fractures with pins and frame.

She was in the hospital for a long time but eventually recovered sufficiently to be returned to the care of her relatives. She had many continuing problems on discharge and faced a long road to satisfactory recovery. We never saw her again after she went home and I do not know the finish of her story. This is one of the frustrations of treating local civilians in a military hospital. Did our efforts survive the dangers of the shift back to domestic life? Would longer hospital treatment have increased her difficulty in adapting back to her home? Did we help her or did we harm her? These answers cannot be answered without follow-up, but follow-up was not possible and, even if it were, it would have put her in further danger from the gentlemen who threw the original bomb.

High-velocity gunshot wounds (HVGSW) may create only one wound but it can be devastating. Wounds to the head, chest or abdomen are usually rapidly fatal. My role as an orthopaedic surgeon was to treat these terrible wounds in the limbs. In Iraq, a young coalition soldier was admitted after being shot just above the knee by an insurgent with an AK47. The entrance wound on the outer side of the thigh just above the knee was about 1 cm across. The bullet had struck the hard surface of the thighbone and both bullet and bone had immediately disintegrated causing a spray of fast-moving fragments to explode out through the inner aspect of the thigh, leaving an exit wound which was 12 cm across and a similar gap in the thighbone. The muscle was mutilated and dead above and below the wound. All nerves and arteries had been divided with large gaps between the ends. The limb was not salvageable and so was amputated above the knee before the casualty was transferred back to a military hospital in the USA.

Iraqi civilians suffered similar injuries. Surgical treatment consists of two stages. Initial wound surgery means cleaning the wound of dead tissue such as skin and muscle, removing contamination such as dirt, clothing and fragments and then stabilising fractures with fixation frames. Reconstruction surgery is the second stage and consists of restoring the best possible function to the limb after 'initial wound surgery' has produced a limb that will tolerate major surgery. Military personnel on deployment were transferred home for reconstructive surgery after their initial wound surgery. Wounded local civilians remained in hospital after their initial wound surgery and we continued with their reconstructive surgery.

One such civilian was shot through the forearm with damage to muscle but with no damage to nerves or arteries and only a simple fracture with no fragmentation. The entrance wound was 2 cm across and the exit wound was 4 cm across. After the initial wound surgery, there was a large 5 cm hole clear through the forearm which was most unattractive. It was possible to look through the forearm from one side to the other as if it was a knothole in the branch of a tree. After dressings and reconstructive surgery, the wound closed in, skin grafts were used to achieve final healing and he was discharged with good function in his arm.

My deployment to Rwanda occurred about 12 months after battles between Hutu and Tutsi that had resulted in large numbers of gunshot wounds that were not treated but allowed to simply heal and recover as best they could. Consequently, it was possible to see the long-term results following a gunshot wound. One unfortunate young man had been shot in the upper arm resulting in a severe fracture to the humerus bone in the upper arm. The bone had fragmented and exploded out through the exit wound. Almost all of the bone had disappeared except for a little bit at the shoulder end and a little bit at the elbow end. There had been no damage to nerves or arteries and so the forearm and hand were normal and had full function but the arm itself was useless because it just hung limply by his side. It was only connected to his body by a thin, floppy bit of skin in the upper arm. His functioning hand either hung uselessly at his side or he put it in his pocket by using his opposite arm so that it did not flop around. He was unable to move the arm in such a way to localise the hand in any useful position. All of his severe wounds had healed but the absence of the humerus had destroyed all function in the shot limb.

The military casualties presenting during the deployment to Balad, Iraq, contrasted to the military casualties in Rwanda because the Iraqi conflict was current and the casualties were immediate. There were 3,800 presentations to the Emergency Department in Balad during the four months that I was there. 1,500 of these patients were admitted and 1,340 proceeded to surgery. A total of 2,390 operations were performed. The vast majority were battle injuries.

I operated on 128 patients during my deployment and did 186 operations because most casualties had multiple injuries and needed repeated operations. The 128 patients had a total of 233 limbs that needed surgical treatment. Multiple limbs had surgery at the one sitting. Eighty-four per cent of these patients had suffered battle injuries and sixteen per cent had suffered civilian style accidents such as sporting injuries, car accidents or work injuries. About 70% of the battle injuries were from IEDs and about 25% were high-velocity gunshot wounds. The remainder had assorted wounds such as rocket-propelled grenades, anti-personnel mine, flare, knife and a dog bite. About 50% of the battlefield injuries were suffered by coalition forces, predominantly US military, and about 50% were Iraqi citizens with a mixture of Iraqi security forces and civilians. There were 114 major fractures that were threatening the survival of the limb because of the damage to skin, blood vessels and nerves. I amputated twenty-eight limbs, twenty-three lower and five upper limbs. The lower limbs were evenly distributed from the foot, to around the knee and as high as a hip disarticulation. Three of the upper limb amputations were at shoulder level.

Forty-six of the severely injured limbs were preserved by applying an external fixator consisting of pins penetrating bone and held together with an external frame. This has the advantages of keeping the broken bones in the best position, it is relatively comfortable for the patient and it is possible to repeatedly change the dressings of severe wounds. Twenty-nine of the fixators were applied to the lower limb and seventeen were applied to the upper limb.

These statistics give an idea of the workload but disguise the human pain and distress of the individual beings. Every single statistic indicates a tragedy for an individual who travels on a rollercoaster of emotions. Firstly, there is the horror of being attacked and confronting death. Then there is the distress of a life-changing injury with either loss of limb or a major wound that is going to take months to recover or may be amputated later. Then there is the relief that the attack has been survived. The comment 'I have lost my leg (or arm) but it could be much worse and at least I am still alive' occurred frequently. The casualties tended to lie quietly and introspectively in bed with thoughts such as 'why did I survive and my buddy got killed', 'I am sorry that this will cause my family so much distress' and 'what does the future hold for me and will I have any further role in the military'.

Chapter 5
Disasters and the Familiar

Treating local citizens living near a military deployment is exciting and satisfying for a deployed orthopaedic surgeon. Medical support for deployed soldiers who are fit and well does not match the professional challenges of complex exotic problems or the satisfaction of treating a population in strife. Treating local citizens relieves boredom when military activity is slow.

The types of treatment required vary according to circumstances. Local civilians may be injured by a devastating natural disaster that has hit their homeland, they may be trapped as 'collateral damage' in military action or they may simply need routine medical care that is not available in their country. Often there is a mixture of all this.

There are paradoxes when deployed military health workers treat local civilians. Do the few that are treated simply create a depressing contrast to the tens of thousands who remain untreated and are not lucky enough to be close to a foreign military deployment? Will the local medical practitioners be involved or consulted? If not, will this cause offence? Are the sophisticated and expensive medical methods of 'first world' nations appropriate for the civilians of countries in distress? Is follow-up essential and will it be available when the deployment finishes? Will the advanced care provided by the military deployment supplant the local facilities so that they are not stimulated to progress and their development is retarded? Will the military deployment train local health workers? Is it all about the egotistic 'warm inner feeling' personalities of the deployed surgeons?

Injuries seen after a natural disaster are fated by 'natural triage'. Medical assistance is not sitting on the ground at the location of tsunami, earthquake or cyclone waiting for the disaster to happen. It takes twenty-four hours or more for the disaster to be confirmed, an advanced medical team to be put together, deployed and then set up facilities. Meanwhile, the most severely injured survivors have died and the team is left with the casualties with less severe injuries. This contrasts with battlefield injuries in war because the surgical support is already sitting on the ground and prepared and so the most severe injuries are treated within one hour and frequently sooner.

Typical disaster injuries were seen after the Aitape Tsunami in Papua New Guinea in July 1998. I recall a twenty-six-year-old woman with a badly displaced fracture of her forearm and a filthy infected wound of the skin covering the fracture, theoretically not life-threatening but with the potential for loss of life or limb if the infection turns to gas gangrene or tetanus. She had similar soiled and messy wounds on her legs which also had the potential for disaster. Contamination with coral is a potent cause of infection. Being caught in a tsunami has been compared with being in a huge washing machine filled with coral, stones, plants, tree branches and any other rubbish which may be around. This woman had not had major injuries to the chest or abdominal organs and had not suffered a head injury otherwise she would not have survived the 24–48 hour wait for treatment. There were many casualties with similar limb injuries but no major organ damage. The victims with internal organ injuries had died before help had arrived but the limb injuries had survived and needed an orthopaedic surgeon.

Treatment for this woman's injuries consisted of widespread removal of the dead and contaminated skin and muscle. The broken forearm bones were pushed and pulled into the best possible position and held with a plaster cast. There is no place for using plates and screws or any other form of metalwork because it will become infected and cause even more trouble.

Many routine orthopaedic cases were treated during the deployment to Rwanda. Theoretically, it was a 'third world' country but that term underrates the facilities and medical staff that existed before the horrendous massacres that occurred in 1994 and 1995. Hospitals had been trashed and doctors and nurses had been murdered and so routine treatment for local civilians had stopped. Our surgical team had the opportunity to help in a small way in our own 'hospital' and also to visit the local 'public' hospital to assist the surgeons. In fact, the local surgeons had a good sense of what was practical and possible in their straitened circumstances and I found their advice useful and important.

Examples of routine orthopaedic cases in Rwanda were correction of a clubfoot in a four-year-old, removal of a large segment of dead bone from the forearm of an eight-year-old with chronic osteomyelitis, correction of a deformed hand following nerve damage that had occurred many years previously and straightening of shinbones of a six-year-old with severe bowlegs. This latter is technically described as bilateral high tibial osteotomies in Blount's Disease.

Some of the most distressing cases found on deployment were local civilians who were 'collateral' victims of military action or deliberate terrorist missions such as suicide bombers. There were cases such as these on almost all of my deployments. The most savage attacks occurred during my deployment to the USAF military hospital in Iraq and this was where I experienced the most severe injuries. Some victims had a single devastating wound from a high-velocity rifle. Others had multiple wounds to multiple systems and limbs due to blast injuries from improvised bombs.

A particularly tragic case was a late middle-aged Iraqi civilian who was admitted to the hospital on my first day of work in Iraq when his relatives dumped him out of a car at the entrance of the hospital and then drove off. Hospital staff found a bombing victim who had been desperately injured with multiple wounds while simply walking down the street at the wrong time when the bomb went off. He had fractures to the bones of his right thigh and his left forearm and elbow. There were gross, contaminated wounds over the fractures with protruding bone at each fracture. The bomb had showered him with a multitude of stones which had penetrated him at high speed causing many holes in his skin like a colander all over his body. Black humour demanded that he was nicknamed 'Mr Pepper Shaker'. The stones had penetrated his face and one eye was blinded. Stones had penetrated his chest, causing a collapsed lung that needed a drain inserted. His bowel was damaged by the blast of the explosion and was leaking bowel contents into his abdomen so that it needed opening and repair and removal of part of his bowel. He was treated by an abdominal surgeon, thoracic surgeon, eye surgeon, neurosurgeon and orthopaedic surgeon. He later developed kidney failure and needed amputation of his left leg through the fracture in the thigh. He was still in hospital but appeared to be surviving at the time that I completed my deployment and left the country. Multiple injuries to multiple body systems and multiple limbs requiring multiple numbers of surgeons is a common story after a bomb blast.

The routine or normal health needs of a civilian population do not stop because there has been a natural disaster. Domestic accidents, infective diseases, cardiac conditions and the whole spectrum of medical problems remain business as usual. Pregnant women continue to have babies. The local medical resources may have been devastated by the disaster and so the deployed military health team are often required to fill the gap and provide continuing care for patients currently undergoing treatment. This is combined with the treatment of acute casualties who have survived the disaster. This extension of care can create problems. Military hospitals do not usually carry the equipment, drugs and expertise for the treatment of chronic civilian illnesses, particularly for the treatment of children and pregnant women. When should care be returned to the local medical services? Sometimes the deployed military hospital provides better care with better equipment and facilities than was available before their arrival at the disaster. There can be a reluctance by the local population to return to their own services because they perceive them as inferior and this can delay resumption of normal services. The deployed military team can find themselves becoming the de facto public health service of the host nation.

Casualties arriving after military conflict are different from casualties received on humanitarian assistance deployments or after natural disasters. They are 'hot off the press' so to speak. They have survived the instant they were wounded but they will die within the next few hours if they are not resuscitated and treated.

The wounds suffered during a natural disaster have similarities to those suffered on the battlefield. The casualties need urgent treatment to survive but will perish before the doctors, nurses and their support arrive on the scene.

This heavily influences the type of casualty treated in each situation.

The military doctor treating casualties from the battlefield will receive numbers of desperately ill patients with life-threatening wounds. Some will have single massive wounds to vital organs. Some will have multiple wounds to multiple limbs and body systems. Many need immediate treatment and it has to be the right treatment and it must be based on an accurate diagnosis. All this is done with minimum facilities in a canvas hospital, in a hostile environment, with stressful urgency and frequently with an overwhelming number of casualties.

The doctor sent on humanitarian assistance to a non-military disaster does not arrive in time to treat the acute severe injuries. They are already dead and the health team faces the issues of clearing the dead, de-contaminating a site for the medical facility (sometimes by commandeering a pre-existing but damaged hospital or clinic) and establishing essential infrastructure such as shelter, clean water, sanitation and safe food supplies. Generally, the deploying health team brings this infrastructure and must provide their own transport that is capable of reaching remote and inaccessible locations. This is why the task is always allocated to the military. Civilian resources do not have the ability to transport the paraphernalia of a hospital, put it on a bare patch of unwelcoming earth and then provide it with shelter, water, sanitation and food.

Treatment of casualties starts before the facility is ready to go. A small number of doctors and nurses get information on number and type of casualties. Some can be helped by simple early treatment. Others are critically injured. They are still alive but are past survival and will tragically slide into the group who were too severely injured to be helped by the arriving medical team. Paradoxically the remaining casualties have relatively less severe injuries that are not immediately life-threatening but will cause death or severe disability within a few weeks if left untreated. Typically these injuries are limb fractures with dirty wounds that will become infected over the next few weeks unless cleaned and dressed. The most feared infections are gas gangrene and tetanus.

There will also be a large number of relatively minor wounds that need cleaning and dressing. These are less urgent but are also a drain on personnel and resources. The team will most likely have brought a limited number of dressings, fluid to wash wounds and antibiotics, and so re-supply becomes a problem. Only a military organisation has the resources and transport options to re-supply.

The disaster has probably put local hospitals out of action and so the deployed facility may be the major health supplier. Local routine medical cases will divert from their wiped-out local hospital to the military hospital causing the workload to increase and distract from the urgent cases presenting because of the natural disaster.

Chapter 6
Surgeon's Comfort Zone

I am an orthopaedic surgeon and, like all medical specialists, my field and area of expertise in my civilian practice became more selective and narrower over the years. One definition of a specialist is someone who knows more and more about less and less until he knows everything about nothing. The opposite occurs while on military deployment. It could be said that a military surgeon knows less and less about more and more until he knows nothing about everything.

An ADF surgical team includes general surgeon and orthopaedic surgeon for surgical procedures. This contrasts with any average sized civilian hospital staffed by many different specialists who know almost everything within their narrow area of expertise. The deployed ADF surgeons must expand their territory into those of other specialists. If this happened in civilian practice, it would be resisted as an 'invasion of my patch' by other specialists. The end result is that deployed military surgeons can be required to operate on cases removed from their comfort and experience. However, they can take solace from knowing that they are the only option available and the alternative for the injured or sick patient is no treatment at all or, worse still, treatment from an unqualified or incompetent fraud.

I experienced this dilemma of operating outside my expertise and comfort zone on a number of occasions and I recall two particularly illustrative cases.

A pregnant woman presented to the ADF hospital in Bougainville distressed because she had commenced labour and she had what is described as an obstructive labour. The baby was coming out the incorrect way, had become stuck and was not intending to progress any further. She needed urgent Caesarean section. The local midwives were experienced and competent but did not have the training or resources to proceed to the level of Caesarean section but certainly were clever enough to know that it was necessary. The only option for the ten years before the arrival of the Peace Monitoring Group was to let nature take its course. This would have meant certain death for the baby and a high risk of death for the mother.

I was the only surgeon available and all looked to me to save the day. I had never done a Caesarean section in my life though I had assisted at a large number during my formative medical years and had experience in abdominal surgery during my time as a general surgical registrar in my early surgical training. This gave me enough confidence to commence. The only reason the end result was successful was because of the guidance by the anaesthetist. To my great fortune, he had worked as a general practitioner in an African third world country many years previously and his duties had consisted of combined anaesthetics and obstetrics, including Caesarean sections. He was accustomed to anaesthetising the pregnant mother, delegating the anaesthetic to a nurse and then proceeding to the surgery. In retrospect, I should have swallowed my surgical pride and acted as anaesthetist while he performed the surgery but I conformed to my responsibilities as a surgeon and probably also conformed to my personality as a surgeon. The anaesthetist watched carefully from his end of the table and gave me wonderful advice and guidance as I proceeded. His help was the difference between success and disaster. The happy end result was a healthy mother and child who were both in a better condition than the mentally traumatised surgeon.

The result of the second case was tragic and distressing. It was during my first deployment to East Timor. The INTERFET hospital was informed of a twelve-year-old boy who had fallen out of a tree and had suffered a head injury. There was concern that he was becoming drowsy and appeared to be getting worse. He was in a remote location and so a helicopter was deployed with our intensive care specialist to evacuate him back to the hospital. He was semi-comatose on arrival and was getting worse. Within a few hours, one pupil had enlarged and stayed that way. This is a sign of a desperately ill patient who has increasing pressure in his skull due to bleeding and swelling of the brain. There is an urgent need for immediate surgery to drill holes in the skull and remove part of the skull to relieve the pressure on the brain. Successful surgery is lifesaving. Unsuccessful surgery or no surgery usually means death or severe disability at best.

Two surgeons were available. One was an obstetrician and gynaecologist who had sub-specialised in gynaecological cancer surgery and was vastly experienced in abdominal surgery and other forms of general surgery but had done almost no neurosurgery. The other was myself who was an orthopaedic surgeon but had spent six months in a brain injury unit during my training many years previously. This rather tenuous experience was enough to get me the responsibility to save the young man's life.

There was no happy ending. The swelling was already desperately severe and decompression was impossible no matter how much skull was removed. The brain had swollen to about three times the size of the carrying capacity of the skull and had passed the stage of salvageable decompression. Military communications back to the home country are good and we were able to discuss the situation with a neurosurgeon in Sydney. The advice was that the opportunity for successful surgery had passed before his arrival at our hospital and the poor boy's life had ended at a tragically young age. The operation was tidied up and completed. The boy had general supportive treatment and eventually passed away during the night.

His immediate family were devastated. They were accepting and not at all critical but disappointed that the team of doctors all the way from Australia had not been able to save their child.

There was an inevitable blow to the morale of the hospital staff.

I also felt bad about it. Deaths during surgery in orthopaedics are unusual and almost never if a child is the patient. It was an unfamiliar outcome for me and I did not like it.

Several years later, I was deployed to a large USAF hospital in Iraq with all specialities covered including neurosurgery. The US neurosurgeon was concerned about head injuries being treated surgically by general surgeons without the benefit of modern investigations such as CT scans. He advised that the type of surgery that I had performed should not be done unless a CT scan has been performed, which was obviously impossible in our situation in East Timor. He advised that otherwise there should be no surgery but non-surgical treatment such as postural treatment (head up), rapid artificial ventilation to increase oxygen and diuretics to get rid of excess fluid. He stated that the success rate for a non-neurosurgeon operating without CT scan availability was about 20% which is about the same if no surgery is performed.

The Australian intensive care specialist who was deployed with me did not agree with this opinion. She was on her first deployment and was enjoying the emotion of plying her trade in such a challenging environment. She had adapted to be a supportive member of the team only with the assistance of her husband posting her regular supplies of home comforts such as reading material and special food requirements. Her opinion on surgery on head injuries was based on her own experience in a large trauma hospital in remote Australia which was staffed by general surgeons but not neurosurgeons. The general surgeons were experienced in surgery on head injuries, they had CT scans available and they consulted neurosurgeons by telecommunication. She stated that they got good results and I have no reason to disbelieve her. There is a message here about the differences in the health systems in Australia and the USA. Australian surgeons tend to be broader trained and skilled while American surgeons tend to be narrower in their skills and are much less willing to depart from their comfort zone.

Chapter 7
Recruitment and Early Years

In 1983, I had been appointed as a visiting medical officer orthopaedic surgeon working at the new Mount Druitt Hospital in western Sydney. This coincided with a period of time when there were unhappy relationships between the NSW Department of Health, public hospital administrators and orthopaedic surgeons working in public hospitals. The climax was the 'Doctors' Medicare Dispute' when many of us resigned on matters of principle. The end result was that working in a public hospital became acrimonious, adversarial, ideological and not enjoyable.

I was keen to find more harmonious work and discussed this with a colleague at one of the Australian Orthopaedic Association medico-political meetings which had been convened as a response to the 'Doctors' Dispute'. The colleague was Dr Barry Collins who had been in the regular Australian Army and had served in Vietnam as a Medical Officer. He had remained in the Australian Army Reserve and had trained as an orthopaedic surgeon on completion of his full-time active service. He had a big personality that was jovial, blunt, practical and forthright. He was supportive of new orthopaedic surgeons coming onto the local scene in western Sydney and his advice was to work as a civilian contractor at the Army base in Ingleburn which was in south-west Sydney. He stated that the Australian Defence Force was looking for surgeons to treat their members and they treated the medical profession with respect and appreciation in contrast to the public hospitals.

I had a look at the Army in Ingleburn. The unit was called 1 Field Hospital. It had a fixed medical and surgical facility but was also deployable as a mobile facility. The staff were welcoming and keen for me to work there. It looked great fun and I was tempted but it was too far from my home and office.

Barry was army through and through but he also had RAAF connections. He worked as a civilian consultant at 3 Hospital RAAF Base Richmond and so I went out there to have a look because it was much closer to my home and office. It was just as appealing as 1 Field Hospital with equally encouraging staff and so I commenced working as a civilian contractor appointed as an orthopaedic consultant to 3 Hospital RAAF.

I enjoyed it immensely. The patients were full-time active service members of the RAAF and so were generally young, fit and motivated. The consultations, surgery and ward care were disciplined and organised. It was in complete contrast to the disorganisation and the acrimony within public hospitals. When colleagues asked about working in the RAAF hospital, I described it as "the way public hospitals used to be."

I started there in early 1984 and by 1987 was part of the scenery, even though I was still working as a civilian. I had got to look at the RAAF and liked what I saw and the RAAF had had a look at me and apparently liked what they saw.

The big change came in early 1987 when the Commanding Officer of RAAF 3 Hospital approached me. He was a senior Medical Officer ranked Wing Commander. He requested that I join the RAAF Specialist Reserve. He pitched it along the lines of joining an exclusive club with immediate commission with officer rank, snazzy uniform, Officers Mess membership with formal dinners, social mixing with senior officers and free run of the RAAF Base with travel and exciting trips in military aircraft a possibility. The RAAF apparently wanted nothing from me in return. I simply had to continue with my civilian contract work and there would be no changes in my conditions of the contract with remuneration and commitment unchanged. There could be a requirement for minimal training and there was a theoretical possibility that I may be needed for full-time active service at some time, but in 1987 this seemed unlikely. The object was simply to 'formalise' my connection with the RAAF and help me to get more enjoyment from it.

I often recollected this conversation over the course of 10 overseas deployments with a total of 14 months of full-time service in harsh environments, usually in hostile war-like conditions.

I put in the required paperwork in mid-1987. My final recruitment was formalised in late 1988. It was my baptism of fire of the strange way things happen in the Australian Defence Force. The process was convoluted with false channels, obstructions, forms filled out and lost, forms filled out but they were the wrong forms and requirements for interviews at odd times and places. There was concern that I did not know whether my grandmother had visited Russia. It was so different from the RAAF that I experienced when I was working in 3 Hospital that I doubted that it was simply inefficiency. I thought they were getting background information on me from spies or similar covert connections and had come to the conclusion that I was not suitable for recruitment. They did not wish to be so obvious as to tell me directly and had decided to torment me with Kafka-style bureaucracy until I gave up and went away. It became apparent that this assumption was incorrect when I found out that the RAAF is not that clever.

Eventually the second last and vital interview happened in the main recruiting centre in Sydney. It was a congenial formality in contrast to the administrative mayhem that went before. The final interview was meant to be my acceptance authorised by senior RAAF officers at RAAF HQ in RAAF Base Glenbrook which is a beautiful 1920s building in the NSW Blue Mountains that was originally a private residence but then resumed by the government for the RAAF. The discordant work commitments of the senior RAAF officers and me resulted in the final interview being constantly postponed until I received an exasperated call from someone in the chain of recruitment who told me that the interview was not necessary and I was now an officer in the RAAF from about mid-1988. I had the substantive rank of Flight Lieutenant and acting rank of Squadron Leader. Substantive rank is your official level and acting rank provides a level appropriate to your training and seniority in speciality, in my case orthopaedic surgery. I moved up the ranks over the years until I was an acting Group Captain but remained a substantive Flight Lieutenant. Two years before finishing with the

RAAF I was pleased to be given substantive rank as a Group Captain. In 1988, I was told that I would be issued a certificate of the commission sometime in the future. I received it in about 2009.

My early years with the RAAF Specialist Reserve were indeed more social than military. There were drinks in the Officers Mess, congenial dinners in the same location and RAAF education from many people with various roles in a complex organisation. Aviation matters such as aircraft maintenance, meteorology, air traffic control, radio communications, aerial photography, airfield defence, cargo loading complexities and many other specialised air force niches were exposed to my enthrallment. There were occasional opportunity flights which sometimes included an invitation to the flight deck.

The most serious commitments were training courses, though these tended to be enjoyable diversions from my civilian practice.

I attended the Reserve Officers' Familiarisation Course which was a reduction of basic officer training from about three months to one week. It covered topics such as RAAF history, administration, ranks and privilege, mess etiquette, drill and marching, which uniform and how to wear it and (most enjoyable of all) pistol training with a 9 mm Browning pistol. There was a group of six of us on the course and we put the mess training to practical use each night.

We had annual conferences for health specialists in the Specialist Reserve where we learnt RAAF topics with a health linkage such as aviation medicine, aero-medical evacuation, combat wounds, ballistics, air crash investigation, deployable health assets, physical fitness assessment, environmental health on deployment, immunisations and continuing instruction on traditions and 'how to enjoy yourself in the air force'. The latter was put into practical use with a formal 'dining in' on the last night when we all dressed up in formal mess kit and made complete fools of ourselves.

I worked as a 'general duties' Medical Officer on one of the RAAF Bases for two weeks which provided excellent familiarity with the RAAF health system and its interaction with the rest of the RAAF. For example, no matter how serious a medical case you may be treating, it all has to stop and you have to accompany the ambulance when an aircraft has had a fright such as a 'bird strike'.

I learnt that military doctors have two owners. They serve the individual patients who are defence force members and they serve the defence force organisation that 'owns' them. Sometimes these responsibilities are irreconcilable and there is a conflict of interest.

In 1992, I spent two weeks on a military exercise with the Australian Army in the Northern Territory near Katherine. This was my first experience in a military camp with all of the aspects of living in a tent, sleeping on the ground or torturous stretcher, improvised toilets, doubtful food from the limited rations and the necessity to look after yourself and also be part of the team. I learnt more about the army and its similarities and contrasts with the RAAF. I was exposed to the inter-service rivalry which sometimes produces healthy stimulation but can also be destructive. My motivation for attending this exercise was a combination of curiosity and a desire to do something 'genuinely military'. I never looked at it as preparation for future overseas deployments to war zones. Within three years, I was deployed to Rwanda and the preliminary experience of this exercise was invaluable.

This happy and symbiotic relationship with the RAAF changed one day when I was approached and told that there were plans to form several deployable 'surgical teams' consisting of a general surgeon, orthopaedic surgeon and anaesthetist. Was I interested in being one of such a team? Of course I was and so my RAAF career either soared or plummeted, depending on my perception at any particular time.

The deployable surgical teams were formalised at a meeting of a small number of committed specialists in RAAF HQ in RAAF Base Glenbrook in the Blue Mountains of NSW. Decisions were made on the essential pre-requisites necessary for a medical specialist to be deployable. It is interesting that there has been little change from these early decisions over the years. Personal requirements were physical fitness, health, immunisation and family support. RAAF requirements were military training programmes such as basic training in living in the field under combat conditions and austere environments like wet jungle or dry desert, radio and other communications, weapon training and documentation such as official passport and International Committee of Red Cross certificate. Professional requirements for each medical speciality were extra training in military medicine, ability to improvise with limited equipment and facilities, experience and ability to treat a broader range of injuries and diseases than in a conventional civilian practice and training in ADF deployable equipment and casualty management protocols such as triage and evacuation.

The most important result of this meeting was my realisation that deploying to provide orthopaedic surgery services for the ADF would be different from my daily civilian practice. This forewarning allowed me to mentally prepare matters such as personal needs, equipment and to anticipate surgical challenges.

Chapter 8
Getting Ready

Taking a medical specialist out of normal civilian medical practice to be transplanted into the unique environment of a military deployment is not something that can be done easily or quickly. Steps and procedures occur before deployment to an established mission but the scenario changes dramatically if the deployment is a rapid response to a natural disaster or a military crisis. The immediacy of the crisis and the urgency required to get medical specialists on the ground determines the character of the pre-deployment preparation

The majority of my deployments were to an established mission with early notice and enough time to get my medical practice and my family organised before departure.

Generally, I was aware that the RAAF or ADF were getting involved in one of their adventures simply by keeping an eye on current affairs on TV and in the newspapers. I could anticipate an approach from officers about my availability and interest in deploying. The approach could be by telephone, email or simply a casual question in the corridor of one of the military bases I may have been visiting. Sometimes the approach was a general call to all specialists rather than directed to me personally.

I learnt early to say 'yes' to any offer to deploy. The instinct was to think of all the trouble that a deployment would cause, such as inconvenience for my civilian practice, frustration for patients, removal of support for referring general practitioners and loss of continuity of treatment. I would need to arrange locum cover for the practice and arrange cover from neighbouring orthopaedic practices.

The reality was that the patients I left behind in Sydney would continue to get better medical service than the casualties where I was going were getting. I could convince myself that I was doing more good by departing rather than staying.

The same rationalising was not relevant to my administrative staff who were always left with a mess and had to manage the 'feedback' from patients who complained that I was off on another 'holiday'. Hospitals and colleagues such as anaesthetists and physiotherapists were also affected. My income reduced precipitously and my family were put under pressure.

These problems were immediately evident and a reflex response such as "no" or "I will think about it" was the easy option. Things can move quickly in the ADF and a rapid answer was always needed. A sniff of refusal would result in the offer being made to someone else and the opportunity for the deployment would be lost. It soon became apparent to me that saying "yes" was going to cause major hassles but saying "no" would result in bitter regrets from a lost opportunity.

Consequently, whenever I was offered a deployment, I would say "yes" immediately and sort out the mess afterwards.

Having agreed to deploy, the next step was the official confirmation and administrative preparation. This would start as written notification and then a flurry of paperwork and pre-requisites. Revisiting one of these documents entitled PRE-CONCENTRATION ADMINISTRATION brings back memories of the details of requirements and the time needed to put it all together. The list of essential documents was as follows: Official Australian Passport, personal medical documents, International Certificate of Vaccination, personal dental record, Record of Service, pay documents, leave records, two colour public relations photographs in uniform, two spare colour passport photographs dressed in civilian clothes, undertaking to Preserve Official Secrets, Clothing Record, completed overseas documentation checklist, driving licences (civilian and military), ADF ID card and identification (dog) tags. Medical requirements were current immunisation against a myriad of infectious diseases, screening for HIV, prophylactic drugs for malaria and pre-deployment medical and dental examination. There was advice and instruction on equipment, pay, the status of service (Permanent or Reserve), special financial allowances, health and life insurance, exposure to chemical hazards, legal assistance (wills and power of attorney), family support, postal services and need to vote if elections occur while deployed.

The document included a substantial checklist with all boxes ticked and signed off by the Commanding Officer of the unit where the member was permanently posted (22SQN in my case) before proceeding to the next step, which was pre-deployment training in a training unit. I can recall my training occurring at various times in Randwick Army Barracks in Sydney, Robertson Army Barracks in Darwin and Amberley RAAF Base just out of Brisbane.

Having arrived for pre-deployment training, the first step was to go through the PRE-CONCENTRATION ADMINISTRATION checklist again and to ensure that all the boxes were ticked (again). It was confirmed that we were currently equipped with combat camouflage uniforms, backpacks, webbing, sleeping bags, ration preparation equipment, eating utensils and weapons (rifle or pistol or both). It was checked that we were current in personal welfare (health and family), personal administration (everything under the sun) and medical and dental health. We had further medical examinations and vaccinations if necessary. We dipped our clothes, sleeping bags and mosquito nets in Permethrin to keep the malaria-toting mozzies away. Instructional lectures and briefs covered Conditions of Service, Pay and Allowances, Country and Cultural (on host country of deployment), Health Awareness, Welfare, Deployment and Separation by Psychologist, Peace Support Operations, Situation in Host Country, Current Intelligence and Operations, Basic Language of Host Country, Customs, AQIS, Arrival in Country, Legal (Rules of Engagement/Orders for Opening Fire) and Logistics of Deployment. We also went to the rifle range to fire our weapons and get the rifle sights adjusted for compatibility with the idiosyncrasies of our individual shooting techniques. The full course lasted one or two weeks.

At the end of all this, we were deemed deployable. We were given a day or two to catch our breath and then bundled into some sort of transport, usually a C130 Hercules, and sent off to our new home for the next few weeks or months.

The pre-deployment training was getting a bit repetitive by the fifth or sixth time and so I began to develop protective methods to reduce the time required. I listed some of the information that I had heard several times and requested that I be exempted from these briefings. I tried to limit my course to equipment issuing and weapon handling and shooting but some topics were regarded as essential and so I was only partially successful. I was congratulating myself on my world-wise experience in the military until I saw the remarkable success along similar lines by one of my anaesthetic colleagues. The only part of the course that he attended was the weapon handling and shooting at the range. He did not even attend the issuing of equipment or weapons. The head instructor picked him up from the airport on his arrival and drove him directly to the rifle range. I first became aware of this when I heard him shouting my name in greeting and waving to me. He had just alighted from the instructor's Land Cruiser and, in the background, I could see the senior instructor preparing a rifle for issuing. He had reduced the training course from seven days to one day by cunningly calculating that an anaesthetist was essential and they would let him get away with it.

This lengthy preparation was in complete contrast to deployments that occurred in response to any crisis that required deployment with less than 24 hours of notification. Deployment then happens without any preparation whatsoever. It was essential to keep yourself equipped and be always able to tick off the boxes for deployment because the call could come at any time.

Chapter 9
Getting There

Deployment to the overseas posting usually occurs within a few days to two weeks after pre-deployment training. Theoretically, it can occur months after the training but, in practice, it usually occurs soon afterwards and the travel arrangements are instructed during the training.

Lockheed C130 Hercules aircraft were prominent in my deployments and these workaholic roustabouts, fondly nicknamed a 'Herc', must qualify as one of the most successful aircraft designs in the history of aviation. They have achieved all that has been asked of them and quite a bit extra. The first test flight of a C130 was in 1955 and, 60 years later, they are as essential and versatile as ever. They can be configured for many different purposes from major cargo transport to personnel deployment. They can be a half and half combination of the two. They can be configured for transport of walking, sitting, and stretcher casualties including those who need intensive care support. They can be long haul or short-haul, strategic or tactical. They are not out of place in the major airports of the world and they can land on short airstrips that are unsealed and without air traffic control. Lengthy routine take-off procedures are accepted protocol but, if necessary, they can be started, warmed-up and take off within minutes. Military personnel dependent on them develop a warm affection for this charismatic aircraft. The sight of the familiar squat fuselage arriving to take you home after a deployment is an emotional moment.

This is not to say that they are comfortable for human passengers. In my civilian travel, I have saved a lot of money by flying economy rather than business class unlike many of my medical specialist colleagues who find economy travel an intolerable torment. I always kept quiet about my air travel habits when these matters were discussed in detail in the tearooms of civilian hospitals. My opinion is that you have to spend many long flights in a C130 to appreciate the luxury of travelling in economy. Note that the airlines call it "Economy" and not "Economy Class" as distinct from "Business Class" and "First Class". I presume they have decided there is no class in economy.

Travelling in a "Herc" means sitting on a sheet of fine-woven plastic netting stretched between two light metal struts and leaning back against plastic webbing that is either too tight or too loose. It is better than it sounds but nowhere near the comfort of economy on a civilian flight. You sit sideways along the side of the fuselage and so you rock to the left and rock to the right depending on the rock and roll motion of the aircraft and its tendency to buck and heave. Hopefully, the aircraft is empty enough for no one to be sitting opposite. If there is, they will be situated so close that both of you keep your knees bent in the limited gap between you to keep the clash of kneecaps to a minimum. The person opposite cannot compensate for this discomfort by being an entertaining conversationalist because the noise of the aircraft and the necessity for earplugs means that conversing is impossible. Reading is just possible despite the movement of the aircraft and the limited light. The greatest mercy is if the aircraft is also carrying cargo because that will be strapped onto a pallet next to the passengers in the tail end of the aircraft. Kind loadmasters will allow you to climb to the top of the cargo and lie down to a recurring sequence of being rocked to sleep and then being jolted awake.

Eight of my ten deployments involved a flight in a "Herc" on at least part of the journey. Some of these were for the full journey and some for just the final leg in or the first leg out. The longest flights were close to nine or ten hours and the shortest were little more than an hour.

One of the most interesting segments was from Kuwait to Balad in Iraq. It was well known that there were still many insurgents in Iraq and they were armed with high-powered rifles and surface-to-air missiles. They took pot-shots at low flying aircraft with little success except for putting the occasional bullet hole in the wing or tail plane. Nonetheless, it was an uncomfortable feeling, especially as a desperately unlucky civilian contractor had been shot dead in a RAAF "Herc" by a bullet fired from the ground shortly before my deployment. We were ordered to don body armour and helmets as soon as we crossed the border from Kuwait to Iraq. There was a little discussion as to whether we were better off sitting on the armour or helmet rather than wearing it as the bullets would be coming up from below.

The insurgents had got surface-to-air missiles from the defeated Iraqi army and from Afghan mujahideen fighters who had been issued the missiles by the CIA during the 1980s occupation of Afghanistan by the Soviet Union. Fortunately, the missiles had become unserviceable with age and lack of maintenance. The insurgents had not mastered the technology of the missile launchers and so were able to switch them on and threaten with them but were not actually able to fire them. The missile sights were radar-controlled direction finders and these always set off the warning electronics on the 'Hercs' whenever the sights were 'locked' onto the aircraft. This required avoidance manoeuvres such as alteration of altitude and course which could make the flight a little bumpier for the passengers. Some aircraft were able to reply to the missile's electronics with countering electronics and so confuse the missile launcher. The threat of a surface-to-air missile was usually dismissed as minimal but attitudes changed during my deployment to Iraq when a British RAF C130 crashed between Balad and Baghdad. We never found out the cause of the crash but the rumour mill went into overdrive and surface-to-air missiles figured heavily in the rumours.

Flying over insurgent occupied Iraq and then landing at insurgent infested Balad required special tactical precautions by the RAAF aircrew. Flying across the country was at low altitude to minimise the chances of hostile characters getting an easy shot at us with rifle or missile. The theory was that we would appear and be gone before they had a chance to get organised. Similarly, the course was somewhat zig-zag so that they could not warn comrades down the flight track who could then be ready and waiting for us. Approach to the airfield and landing were also done at a somewhat higher speed with less preparatory manoeuvres.

This contrasted with the technique used by the US Air Force. They maintained a high altitude across the country so that they were out of range from everything until they were over the base. They would then descend rapidly in a spiral fashion and land relatively quickly.

The first leg of travel from Australia was frequently in civilian commercial airlines, such as Qantas, and then military transport for the second and third legs. The trip to Rwanda was Qantas to Johannesburg and then South African Airways to Nairobi. The next leg was a UN-chartered C130 flown by an Italian company. This was my first scary experience of the UN taking the cheapest option with little care about the impact on personnel under their wing. The sad appearing C130 had been beaten up but was deemed serviceable. It got us to Kigali but only after some administrative hiccups. Our Australian surgical team was not on the passenger manifesto and we were informed that we would not be able to board. We were allowed to sit around for a while in case there were some 'no-shows'. In the event, 25 people did not turn up and so off we went.

We landed at Kigali Airport, which looked as though it had been quite a luxurious establishment at one stage. It was constructed of quality tiled floor and walls. There was an up-market souvenir shop and glass cases displaying stuffed native animals and museum artefacts. At one stage, it had been better appointed than Nairobi Airport, probably because of the influence of the Belgian airline, Sabena, which had used it as a key hub of their African services and so provided top quality facilities for customers and crew. Unfortunately, any pleasing aspects of the airport had been totally trashed by innumerable bullets fired off during the violence that had occurred throughout the troubled country's recent past. The glass cases had been smashed, the stuffed animals were tattered and the souvenir shop was a mess of broken glass and timber. The walls and ceilings were covered with pockmarks from bullets. There was debris all over the floor. Doors and windows were smashed or had been removed leaving gaping holes in the walls.

This UN flying experience was not as bad as that experienced by other ADF personnel entering Rwanda. There was talk of a Russian aircraft with Russian aircrew but no cabin crew. It had UN markings and was described as being in a dilapidated condition that was the equal of our Italian C130. The overhead lockers had a tendency to shed bits and pieces during flight. There was a little concern that there were no seatbelts. Apparently, one of the Nursing Officers mentioned this to the pilot when he unwisely made a personal appearance. He confirmed there would be no seatbelts. She asked for his anticipated result if the aircraft crashed. She saw a wide, beaming Russian smile with wall-to-wall gold teeth. He informed her, "We all die". They gave him full marks for realism.

C130s were the allocated aircraft for the full trip for five of my deployments, specifically from Australia to Vanimo (Papua New Guinea) at the time of the tsunami, from Australia to Bougainville, from Australia to East Timor for the second and third deployments and from Australia to the Solomon Islands.

Vanimo was chosen as the destination because the airfield was closest to the disaster area and had a runway that was sealed and long enough. It was also close to logistic facilities such as accommodation, power, undamaged roads and buildings available for supplies and patient care. There were other airfields closer to the disaster area but they were unsealed, probably damaged by the tsunami and there was doubt as to whether any logistic facilities had survived.

The flight to Bougainville was long but was relatively comfortable and uneventful. We landed on a primitive unsealed runway that was on privately owned land. It was necessary for the 'Herc' to do one or two dummy runs over the runway to frighten off all of the livestock that were wandering around and alert the owner who was nicknamed 'Bob Marley'.

The flight to the Solomon Islands was particularly interesting, not least because I was seated in the flight deck and had a great view of the archipelago of this beautiful South Pacific island nation. I was able to appreciate the significance of landing at the historic Henderson Airport that services Honiara on Guadalcanal. It was originally built by the Japanese in World War 2 but was almost immediately captured by the United States. They re-named it Henderson Airfield in honour of United States Marine Corps Major Lofton Henderson, who was killed during the Battle of Midway while leading his squadron into action against the Japanese carrier forces, thereby becoming the first Marine aviator to perish during the battle. The airfield was enormously significant, strategically, tactically and symbolically, and was the prize that was fought over in the prolonged and bitter campaign known as the Battle of Guadalcanal. The US and allies eventually succeeded and it was the first time that the Japanese were defeated in a major campaign and expelled from occupied territory. It was a turning point in the war in the Pacific.

The first flight to East Timor was from Darwin in an aircraft that looked like a 'mini-Herc' with two engines. I never found out what it was. It was flown by Italians and I never found out who they were either. They may have been Italian air force or may have been civilian contractors. The flight was the same as being in a normal 'Herc' but with a shorter fuselage. The second flight to East Timor was in a 'Herc' with UN markings on the fuselage and flown by South Africans. The aircraft was in good condition by UN standards. It had been fitted with standard airliner seats facing forwards and not plastic netting. We were issued rifles in Darwin and there was a bit of administrative rigmarole to get them checked onto the aircraft. The third flight to East Timor was again in a UN C130 and again we had to go to Ansett Airlines to check in our weapons.

The flight to Kuwait during the journey to Balad, Iraq, should have been straightforward. The ADF arranged commercial flights on a civilian airline to arrive in Kuwait and then military aircraft to Balad. My situation was more complicated because I had already arranged to attend a Society of Military Orthopaedic Surgeons (SOMOS) conference in Vail, USA. SOMOS is a US-based organisation for the education and other benefits for US orthopaedic surgeons with a military connection. Most members are in active military service but a significant number are also in full-time civilian practice. There are a small number of members from countries other than the US. The educational and social benefits for an ADF member such as myself are considerable. I had committed to the conference before I learnt of my deployment to Iraq and my wife and I had also booked skiing in Canada and France to follow the conference. We did not want to cancel our trip and so I asked permission from the ADF to make my own travel arrangements to Kuwait. There was considerable reluctance and concern by the ADF administration because they are accustomed to totally organise members and any show of independence makes them uneasy. Finally, it was agreed that I would get myself to Geneva on a certain date and they would fly me from there to Kuwait.

Their reluctance was justified when I fell during my first run on my first skiing day in Vail and fractured my ankle. There was no more skiing for the remainder of the six-week trip and the time was used to rehabilitate my ankle sufficiently to complete the deployment. I also put considerable effort into disinformation to hide the true situation from the important decision-making people back in Australia. This was done successfully and the deployment proceeded with my ankle functioning normally despite the severity of the recent injury. The trip was enjoyable because of the quality of the SOMOS conference and because of the enjoyment my wife experienced while skiing in Vail, Mont Tremblant and Bourg Saint Maurice, enjoyment possibly enhanced by my absence from the slopes.

By the time of my deployment to Afghanistan, the ADF had so many personnel going back and forth to the Middle East that they had chartered an Airbus A330-300 owned and operated by a Portuguese company known as Strategic Airlift. I travelled in Business Class! It did not make much difference because the economy end of the aircraft was one-third occupied and would have been just as comfortable. The economy occupants stretched out over four seats and slept soundly. We transited through the Maldives and then went directly to Kuwait. We had a repeat of our pre-deployment training in Kuwait and then on to Tarin Kowt in Afghanistan in a RAAF C130. The flight precautions were the same as when we flew into Balad. We landed on the unsealed runway in Tarin Kowt in huge clouds of dust. The unsealed runway could be a problem. It could be closed because of wind and dust or it could be closed because of rain and mud.

After the aircraft flight came the trip between airfield and deployed unit. The journey over land was just as utilitarian as the journey by air. The medical unit was usually co-located with the airstrip and so the next stage of the journey was a ride in a 4WD vehicle or sitting in the back of a troop truck along a bumpy road with luggage packs falling all over the place. This was our first chance to have a look at our circumstances for the next short while.

Chapter 10
The Military Base

Defence forces can place a large number of people in an empty field and they can be self-sufficient. This is necessary for their survival. The ADF can place hundreds of its members in an empty paddock and provide shelter, security, food, water, toilet sanitation, washing facilities, hygiene, communications and healthcare. No other organisation in Australia can do this and it can be assumed that only the military has this capability in all other countries.

This does not mean these bases are comfortable or aesthetically pleasing places to live. They vary from rough and ready to even more rough and ready. It is always interesting to see the reaction of incoming teams to the environment they find on arrival. I can remember my own thoughts on arrival on each of my three deployments to East Timor and then reading the same thoughts in the faces of the replacement team at the time of my departure. Each time my arrival consisted of landing at Dili airport and immediate road transport to the hospital and accommodation. The first impression was always dust, heat, a society in disarray, humidity and sweat. A feeling of revulsion is inevitable. The first impression of hospital and living conditions was of dirt, discomfort and a deep foreboding that I would not be able to cope with the conditions. Sweat soaked my uniform and settling dust turned the sweat into mud. I would move slowly to preserve my diminishing energy and breathe super-heated air into my lungs. I would struggle to stay standing on my feet while my surgical colleagues in the departing team provided the information during the handover. These were colleagues who were the same as me while we were in Australia and yet I could only marvel at how well they accepted the conditions that I was finding intolerably oppressive. They did not appear to sweat; they moved normally and showed no sign of distress. They made ridiculous statements such as "it is a beautiful day today". They had acclimatised to the tropics, which takes about two to three weeks and is almost imperceptible. I became aware of my acclimatisation when I was leaving and handing over to the arriving team. They would be unable to listen because they were almost collapsing on the spot because of their distress from the heat, humidity and harsh conditions. They would look annoyed with my teasing comment "it is a beautiful day today".

There is a repetitive routine of the arriving team looking at conditions and silently thinking, *this place is a shithole. Here is my esteemed colleague X whom I thought had high standards and yet he is working and living in this shithole. I cannot believe that he has accepted such poor circumstances. I am going to improve this and get it up to standard. There are going to be changes around here.* And indeed, there are improvements which, combined with the acclimatisation to the climate, make life much more tolerable and eventually enjoyable as time progresses. The situation is accepted and the improvements cease sometime before the completion of the deployment. The conditions have improved from rough and ready to not quite as rough and ready. Life is good and the time for departure and the handover arrives. The acclimatised departing team instructs the non-acclimatised arrival team and cannot understand their obvious discomfort and distress. Meanwhile, the new arrivals are silently thinking: *This place is a shithole. Here is my esteemed colleague, Greg Bruce, whom I thought had high standards and yet he is working and living in this shithole. I cannot believe that he has accepted such poor circumstances. I am going to improve this and get it up to standard. There are going to be changes around here.* And so the process is repeated at each arrival of a new surgical team and there are incremental changes but never the final achievement of an acceptable degree of comfort.

I cannot recall ever arriving at my destination for a deployment and thinking that I had entered a pleasing environment. The closest was the Solomon Islands where we were accommodated in a dilapidated and unused holiday resort and in Vanimo, PNG, where we were accommodated in a disused school. Both locales were sufficiently idyllic for a tropical holiday if the deficiencies of the accommodation were ignored. In every other deployment, there was always an impression of dirt, noise, military equipment under stress, temporary buildings which were just coping and vehicles which looked as though they had not been cleaned or maintained for months. Typically, the dust had covered everywhere and everything had turned the same colour as the dust. This effect was accentuated by the camouflage colour patterns of vehicles, buildings, netting and clothing. The whole scene would seem to be in monochrome. The colour of the monochrome was unique to the location. Iraq was a light brown/yellow, Afghanistan was red, Rwanda was brown, and the Solomon Islands were green.

The sizes and activities of the bases varied. As a medical specialist, I could always expect to be posted to the main base which was large enough to support the services required for a surgical medical facility. Nonetheless, facilities could be basic. The smallest was in Vanimo, PNG, where we were deployed to provide medical services after the tragedy of a tsunami that had resulted in thousands of fatalities. This was not a typical deployment because the task of the contingent was to provide medical services directly to civilians. The base consisted of accommodation on stretchers in a disused school, improvised mess facilities in an open area on concrete, communal showers and tents for operating theatre and patient accommodation.

A more typical ADF medical deployment is medical support for deployed military forces on active service. Generally, the surgical services provide base support for the active forces going out into the threatened zones and do not participate in the "pointy end" of military operations. The exceptions are the full-time junior Medical Officers who may be required to accompany combat units such as Special Forces when they are at increased risk of battlefield injuries.

Only the deployments to Iraq and Afghanistan were located in purpose-built military bases. The others were in appropriated civilian facilities, a private hospital in Rwanda, a school in Vanimo, a processing plant in Bougainville, a museum in East Timor and a holiday resort in the Solomon Islands.

The largest base was the USAF base in Balad, Iraq. It was huge, 8km by 8km, and with a population of about 50,000, which was not many fewer than the entire

ADF. It was the main training centre and academy for the Iraqi Air Force during Saddam Hussein's rule and was commandeered by USAF after his defeat. They then used it as their main base for transport and combat aircraft. All shapes and sizes of aircraft arrived and departed at all hours of the day and night, from gigantic Galaxies to tiny piston-engine machines that were dwarfed by a C130. F16 Fighting Falcons departed on patrols at about 5 am each morning, duties which they shared with similar aircraft based outside of Iraq. Their afterburners fired them vertically upwards with a wonderful combination of flame and noise to avoid the risks of a missile attack. There was no need to use an alarm clock to wake in the morning. Helicopters were in abundance and there were all types categorised as utility, cargo and attack.

Supplies for Iraq arrived by air or road convoy and were stored in containers and buildings spread all over the base. Supply dumps were everywhere and their distribution appeared random. Fleets of large earth-moving machinery, cartons of high-tech electronic equipment, food supplies, weapons, ammunition, transport vehicles, disassembled shelters, communication equipment and all of the other paraphernalia needed for a military occupation were lying all over the 25 square miles of the base.

The logistics appeared to be unmanageable but I was convinced otherwise when I was searching for my trunk of personal effects that had not arrived on schedule. The CO of the Australian medical team and I looked around the supply dumps during our unsuccessful search but we appreciated the organisation of the US defence forces. It was remarkable how their personnel had knowledge and documentation of the location of the stores and equipment needed for a medium-sized city.

The supplies stored on Balad Air Base were distributed throughout the country in convoys of a dozen or more huge transport vehicles that departed in the early hours of the morning.

The majority of personnel on base were members of the US defence force and all services were represented. USAF owned and commanded the base. Administration such as the structures and location of facilities was controlled by USAF. They were responsible for security within the base and the perimeter outside the base for a distance of a few kilometres. Air traffic control and movement of all aircraft such as fighters, transporters and helicopters were USAF. The transporters and all other heavy military equipment were owned by the US Army and so there were many army personnel looking after logistics and stores. US Army combat troops were on base to assist in security well beyond the base perimeter and to provide armed escorts for convoys. Army also used the base as a starting point for long distance patrols to combat insurgents and for more major military adventures such as liberating towns and cities that had been taken over by insurgents. A similar role was undertaken by US Marines on base and they were supported by US Navy personnel such as medical support and navy helicopters. All four services of the US defence force were there. Most were full-time active service but there were also a large number of reservists. There were also organisations that were partly military but usually associated with homeland security of the USA, such as Coast Guard and National Guard.

There were pockets of personnel from other countries. Australia had the embedded medical team, of which I was a member, and RAAF had provided a team of air traffic controllers. There were a few personnel from the UK to assist with RAF movements in and out of the largest air base in Iraq. Some eastern European countries had contributed personnel who had been embedded within US units. Presumably, the US had been able to apply some sort of political pressure on these countries to persuade them to contribute. I did not find a major NATO presence, probably because the base was under exclusive US command and not NATO.

There were many civilian contractors, mainly from the Indian subcontinent. Food supplies and mess services had been contracted to a major US supplier linked to Halliburton, a monster sized private company that provided supplies and services to the US defence force. Security personnel recorded the numbers attending for meals with a little clicker. It was rumoured that each click represented a set amount paid by the US Government to the private contractor, allegedly at a value of US$60 for each click. There was no evidence that the clicks had anything to do with payment.

Local Iraqi civilians also came on base as cleaners, laundry workers and labourers. This caused some disquiet amongst the US military and fed the rumour mill, creating stories such as one of the cleaners was an insurgent and had been caught stealing a map of the base. By and large, they appeared to be normal people whose lives and country had been shattered and they were trying to get back on their feet. Working for the Americans was not completely safe. Mortar bombs and rockets kept landing on the base. During my deployment there were several suicide bombing atrocities at the front gate of the base that killed Iraqis queuing up for work.

The base itself was a mixture of images that were fantastic and left long-lasting recollections: many people hustling and bustling everywhere, many types of uniforms and personal weapons, heavy weapons, destroyed Iraqi Army tanks, destroyed Iraqi Air Force MIGs, large machines of warfare, large civilian machines converted for warfare, Humvees left right and centre, stacks of every type of supply imaginable, rough and ready accommodation. Intermingled with this were futile attempts to provide the American comforts of a home from home; eating halls with every possible form of the American style of food, a cinema, regular entertainment, a bus service, coffee shop franchise, huge gymnasium. Everything was covered with fine dust which produced a pervasive monochrome effect. The whole base was a red-brown colour. The maximum use of camouflage clothing, buildings, vehicles and equipment emphasised the effect. Ironically, the main contrast in colour came from Australian eucalypt trees that lined the roads in abundance. The roads were also lined with concrete bunkers where we crept about three times each day when the base was attacked with mortar bombs and rockets. Fortunately, the mortar bombs never hit anything and the rockets usually failed to explode. A huge rubbish dump was constantly on fire and the smoke and smell hung over the base and added to the air of desolation.

There was constant noise; trucks, tanks, heavy earth moving equipment, aircraft, helicopters, shouting, small weapon firing on the rifle range, controlled explosions of captured bombs and IEDs.

Despite all of this, I found it an exciting place to live and left with positive memories of the entire deployment.

My deployment to Afghanistan was also a posting to a major military base adjacent to a strategic and tactical airfield near Tarin Kowt. It was under NATO command and was occupied by defence forces from many different nations. The Netherlands were predominant and had a close partnership with the ADF medical team because the hospital was commanded and administered by the Netherlands. Most of the personnel were Dutch and the Australian ICU and surgical teams were part of the non-Dutch minority. The French and British defence forces were also represented on the base. The US had personnel in an enclave on the base that cooperated with NATO but was under US command. The Americans did not allow their people to be under NATO command and so they needed their own facility with US command and control structures. This decision was probably wise. My impression was that things happened much more quickly and efficiently under the simpler US command protocols in Iraq than under the NATO systems in Afghanistan.

The base consisted of armour-plated strongboxes the size and shape of shipping containers. They were linked to each other in rows with tarpaulins stretched between the rows to provide extra shelter and space. The rows were modified to fulfil their specific function such as accommodation, communications, stores, mess, administration and our hospital. Additional blast protection was provided by arcades of wire netting frames full of large pebbles. There was the customary military activity of vehicle convoys, training, weapon maintenance, drones and helicopters. Artillery was lined up pointing off base for a rapid response to any 'incoming' ordnance.

The runway was unsealed and so all aircraft threw up clouds of light dust that settled on the rest of the base and set the colour scheme for buildings, vehicles and equipment.

The base was 'picturesquely nestled' in the Hindu Kush mountain range and the views were outstanding. We were surrounded on all sides by the red peaks and valleys of classic Afghan mountain terrain with just a hint of remnants of white snow on the tips. The local village could be seen in the closest valley with an intermingling of green trees, red walls and houses. The houses were red cubes shielded by their individual encircling wall.

I deployed to Dili, East Timor, on three occasions and always to the same location at the deployed hospital in the commandeered museum. It was under INTERFET command on the first deployment and under the UN command of UNTAET on the second and third deployments. There was a mixture of personnel from the defence forces of different countries on each occasion but our CO was always a member of the ADF.

The three deployments in East Timor over the same number of years provided an interesting insight into the evolution and maturation of the base. The first deployment was a military force finding a place that was potentially comfortable but meanwhile existence would be primitive and reactive. Resourceful improvisation and security were high priorities. The accommodation was crowded and uncomfortable with washing and toilet facilities to match. The base had no recreation facilities and only basic food and mess provisions. The hospital was in its infancy in a commandeered museum with camp stretchers for beds and a tent for operating theatres. My deployment was in the middle of the wet season which did not improve the comfort level. Other bases in Dili were in much the same state of early gestation. I had the opportunity to visit the units involved in supplies, transport, infantry, aero-medical evacuation, airfield defence and administration. All were faced with sites that had been trashed by militia shortly before the arrival of the ADF and all units had to clean up and make the most of what was available. As a result, everyone was sleeping in wet and dirty circumstances, on bases that were constantly muddy or dusty depending on the vagaries of the wet season. Washing and toilet facilities were limited and food was aimed at survival rather than enjoyment. There were an unexpectedly high number of tropical diseases such as malaria, dengue fever and bowel infections.

There were significant improvements by the time of my second deployment to Dili and the place had the appearance of a permanent military barracks by the time of my third deployment. The accommodation was in demountable buildings, showers were hot, toilets flushed, there was fresh and variable food for meals and we ate on seats with tables in the mess. There was a raised decking area for entertainment and relaxation. The patients had proper beds and the wards were clean. Malaria and dengue fever had been greatly reduced. Problems of water supply, sewerage and waste disposal had greatly improved.

My very first deployment was in Kigali, Rwanda, and we were accommodated in the shattered skeleton of a private hospital. It had been one of the multitudes of sites where Hutu massacred Tutsi and the hospital was almost ruined during the turmoil. Every wall was pockmarked from the impact of bullets and explosives. Nonetheless, the buildings retained some of their basic services and we had intermittent water and power. The main operating theatre was still functional and was appropriated for our use. I had my own room and en-suite toilet. There was good ward accommodation for patients. I did not appreciate it at the time, but it was probably one of my most comfortable deployments.

There was an Australian Army infantry company deployed with us for security. They were based in barracks about one block away and were also fairly comfortable. We used to walk there for recreational activities and some meals, always guarded by a soldier with a Minimi machine gun.

I also had the chance to visit the UN headquarters and accommodation quarters in the old Sabena transit station. Belgium had a major presence in Rwanda before the massacre and so it was an important stopover for their national airline. Sabena had provided luxurious accommodation and facilities for their aircrew and it must have taken the UN a nano-second to find it and move in.

The accommodation in Bougainville was in a huge industrial plant used for processing the raw material from the large mine in the centre of the island which had been the main catalyst for the disagreement between the Papua New Guinea government and the people of Bougainville. The disagreement had lasted for ten years and the mine and the processing plant had stopped functioning for that period of time. The plant was on the coast with port access to prepare the raw material for export by ship. There were two or three gigantic iron buildings and our base was situated under the cover of the buildings. It was the usual tent city for accommodation, hospital, mess, administration, stores, etc. but we had the luxury of a high roof over the tents to provide extra shade during the hot, dry season and protection from rain during the hot, wet season.

Chapter 11
Base Security

The ADF bases were always secured to protect ADF personnel but the steps taken to achieve this varied according to the nature of the deployment and the perceived threat. The two contrasting extremes were the humanitarian assistance deployment to a grateful nation in Vanimo, Papua New Guinea, and the military deployment in Iraq that was deep in the insurgent territory and was supporting patrols that made contact with hostile enemies. Some of these contacts were as close as the front gate.

The deployment to Vanimo was on the invitation of the Papua New Guinea government and this implied that they would provide security and protection. We deployed unarmed and without an escort. Papua New Guinea police and defence force were present. There was never a hint of a threat from the local population who were universally friendly and appreciative of our presence. They gave any assistance possible and then expressed their gratitude with a fascinating and beautiful Sing Sing ceremony just before our departure.

Some of our medics were 'Special Forces' and were usually armed while on deployment. It was rumoured that this may have been the case in Vanimo as 'insurance' but was never confirmed. If so, it was unnecessary insurance. The deployment was secure because of the gratitude and assistance of the local population.

In contrast, we were deep in hostile territory in Balad, a reality celebrated by the USAF CO giving me a certificate that congratulated me on surviving on the "most attacked US base in Iraq". This assessment was made by recording the number of times mortar bombs and rockets landed on the base which averaged about three or four times each day. Sometimes, we had sufficient warning to head for concrete bunkers for cowering duty before the ordnance arrived. Sometimes the warning arrived after the bombs had landed but we still did our cowering, even though it was a bit late and pointless. The mortar bombs exploded but rarely hit anything significant. The rockets were more accurate but rarely exploded. The closest I got to a mortar bomb was about 100 metres and it gave me a huge fright when it went off. I was just getting myself back together when the warning siren sounded and I had to head off to the shelter for cowering. My closest experience with a rocket was one that penetrated the roof of a hospital tent shelter and then landed in a yard next to the hospital entrance. It made a huge pit in the ground but did not explode. It was stuck in the ground with its fins protruding from the pit looking like an amateurish attempt to make a B-grade war movie set.

The rumour mill made merry with the theories as to who was firing at us and how they managed to continue to do so despite the big US military presence outside the perimeter. We had artillery on base that was said to be able to track the incoming ordnance with radar and then immediately return fire accurately to the source of the missile. I was told that the insurgents used several methods to circumvent this danger. They fired from populous areas so that it was too dangerous to return fire because of the risk to innocent civilians. They 'persuaded' local civilians to fire the weapons with payment or threats. I was shown surveillance footage from a drone recording of a Toyota Hilux light truck that drove up to a location, where six men quickly set up a mortar gun next to the truck and then shot off four bombs before they dismantled the gun, put it in the truck and drove off immediately. The whole episode was over in a few minutes and I was told that it was too quick for the defences to return fire. It was assumed that the men were previous members of the Iraqi army because their method was so professional.

The deadliest attacks were just outside the perimeter of the base and usually caused tragic casualties of local civilians who were trying to get some sort of employment inside the base and get their lives back together. The usual weapon was an IED. When I first deployed, the term IED or Improvised Explosive Device was a little-known acronym and I usually had to explain it to friends and colleagues. Now it is so well known that it is a familiar part of everyone's language. Suicide bombers on foot or in vehicles were the preferred method used by insurgents to terrorise their countrymen. Ordinary people who cleaned, carried loads and gardened felt the brunt of these capricious and indiscriminate weapons. Ceremonies for graduating police were particular targets.

The perimeter of the base was a high concrete wall located behind rolls of barbed wire. There were tall watchtowers at regular intervals manned by USAF guards who were armed with heavy machine guns. There was always an armed Blackhawk helicopter flying circuits around the perimeter of the base. Closed circuit television and satellites provided non-stop imaging of the territory outside the wall. Approach roads were especially monitored. The images were relayed into a large room with multiple TV screens that were constantly viewed by security forces. The USAF was responsible for the first few kilometres outside the wire and the US Army was responsible outside of that. Personnel from each service sat in the same room to watch the monitors.

The base in Afghanistan had similar issues. It was also a purpose-built military base participating in armed combat and surrounded by a less than friendly local population. It was encircled by two fortifications. The inner one was the familiar stones in wire frames and was manned by NATO personnel. The outer one did not have the same impregnable look about it and was manned by the local defence forces. The rumour mill aroused fears and insecurities with theories that some of their weapons were pointing inwards. There were also rumours that some of our Afghan defenders had slipped through the fortifications and headed for the insurgents, possibly taking their weapons with them.

We faced a different form of threat during the Rwanda deployment. The sequence of events was started by the massacre of Tutsi by Hutu. Then followed the invasion by the Rwandan Patriotic Front, which was based in Uganda and consisted of Tutsi who had been expelled from the country several years previously by the Hutu. The Front fought and defeated the Hutu forces and gained military control of the country. They changed their name to the Rwandan Patriotic Army

(RPA) and were making noises about a revenge massacre of Hutus. The UN raised a peacekeeping force in the hope that this would not occur but were only partly successful.

Meanwhile, the RPA were frustrated that foreign troops were preventing their vengeance, particularly as they had done the hard work of pacifying the country by force of arms. We could sense their attitude to us of resentful acceptance, but not a friendly welcome. When UN forces interacted with RPA, little incidents occurred that were possibly attempts to provoke a hostile reaction. One example was a minor collision between vehicles that resulted in Australian soldiers having to threaten the RPA with loaded rifles to ensure their vehicle was returned. Our hospital and accommodation were located across the road from an RPA barracks and there was evidence of torture and summary executions being performed to provoke an over-reaction from UN forces. Groups of RPA soldiers used to take training runs on the roads around the hospital. They sang and chanted as they ran and it all sounded appealingly folksy and amicable until we were told, rightly or wrongly, that we were the subject of the chants and their intention was to kill us.

The main threat in Rwanda was the risk of a clash between individuals or small groups and so we were escorted by an Australian Army infantry company whose specific task was security for the medical team. The Tutsi deliberately tested the discipline of the Australian Army on several occasions, notably at the time of the Kibeho massacre. More information on this dreadful incident is available in the book *Pure Massacre* by Kevin O'Halloran.

There were no great security issues with the other deployments. East Timor was dangerous away from the secure areas but this improved with each successive deployment as the UN and civilian government steadily increased their control of the country. I was mainly limited to the base in Dili but did manage to get away on several trips across the country. It was obvious that security decreased when out and about from the main base.

There were no security issues in Bougainville and the Solomon Islands. The main threat was petty crime by a distressed population and we were given instructions on avoidance of problems.

We were issued with personal weapons on all deployments except to Vanimo, PNG, for the tsunami and to Bali after the second bombing. Sometimes we could choose between Steyr rifle and Browning 9mm pistol and my preference was always to take a rifle because I was better trained in its use and it was a safer weapon with better accuracy. The incidence of accidentally firing the weapon was much lower with a rifle. This is called an 'Un-authorised Discharge' or 'UD' and was punishable with a fine equivalent to several weeks work, unless the round had hit someone which would result in criminal charges. The other advantage of a rifle was its effectiveness if needed to be used in anger, in contrast to a 9 mm pistol which was inaccurate and fairly useless. The choice of taking a pistol was theoretically more convenient but the higher incidence of UDs was a big disadvantage.

We kept the weapons at varying degrees of readiness. Sometimes, they were loaded and sometimes they were unloaded. Sometimes, we had to carry them all of the time and at other times, they were locked away near our accommodation or in the armoury. This could vary during the term of a deployment. I was always a bit nervous about having easy availability of such a powerful weapon over a long period of time and I was always pleased to hand it back, relieved that I had not accidentally fired it and caused a terrible injury. In contrast, I enjoyed weapon training when we were issued with rifles for a day or two and were trained in its use and maintenance. I enjoyed the range shooting and improving my marksmanship with the advice of the Airfield Defence Guards at RAAF Base Richmond.

Chapter 12
Personal Comfort and Health

Accommodation could be described in either ascending or descending order of quality and comfort. It is difficult to separate the contenders for most uncomfortable and so I will list them in chronological order.

The ADF medical team in Kigali, Rwanda, were accommodated in the private hospital in the same complex as the wards, operating theatres and supporting health units such as X-rays and laboratory. I was never sure whether we were in a former ward for VIP patients with single rooms and extra facilities or whether we were in former staff accommodation. I believe it was the latter. My room was comfortable with a proper bed, toilet and washbasin with clean but cold running water. I was one of the lucky ones. Everyone had a room but there were few with toilet and washbasin. The shower block was communal and just down the hallway. The controls were unpredictable and the method of manipulating the taps appeared to vary each day. The most engaging feature of the shower was that it could be cold one day and hot the next. One always started the shower optimistically but with preparation to brace if it was one of the cold days. The roller coaster of emotion may have been less stressful if it had been cold every day.

I had a room with a view. I could see rows and rows of washing on clotheslines that was the hard work of the local women employed by the UN. There were military uniforms, bed sheets, patients' clothing, towels, surgical gowns, drapes, dressings and personal clothing. Central Hospital Kigali, the local public hospital, could be seen behind the laundry. It was a short walk up a stone pathway and past Australian Army infantry who manned a machine-gun post between the two hospitals. There was a grassed courtyard adjacent to the laundry where we could relax or undergo courses such as weapon training. The aspect was colourful and appealing, and not completely spoilt by the pockmarks from multiple bullets that had been fired into the buildings during the massacres and civil war.

We had a lounge area and mess in the same building which was on the boundary of the hospital overlooking the road and into the local Rwandan Patriotic Army barracks. Relationships between the RPA and the UN forces were uneasy, to say the least. Our gates were secured by our infantry and there were stories of deliberate abuse of prisoners in full view of our guards, allegedly to induce a reaction that could result in hostile action between the forces. We could also admire the RPA running and chanting their intention to kill us.

The food was good and was prepared by the UN kitchen. It was transported to the hospital for our mess. We also had the option of walking a short distance, escorted by an infantryman, to the main barracks of our infantry where there was a larger mess with a wider choice of meals.

The next deployment to Vanimo, Papua New Guinea, was for humanitarian aid following a tsunami and so it was not as 'warlike' as Rwanda but was much more active and improvised because of the urgent response to a natural disaster.

The accommodation was in a school building with adjacent toilet and shower block. I am not sure if it was a disused building or whether it had been commandeered and the students and staff had been displaced. It was comfortably functional but dilapidated. We all rigged camp stretchers in a large, common area and strung up mosquito nets to keep out the disease-carrying pests and so avoid dreaded malaria and dengue fever. The first few nights on a camp stretcher are miserable. I toss and turn and each movement allows the carefully located sharp angles of the structure maximum opportunity to dig into your most sensitive areas. I usually adapt after about five or six days though I also found sleeping on the ground more comfortable if it was dry and flat.

The toilets were respectable by the standards of later deployments. The showers were hot and steamy to match the hot and steamy climate. The mess was trellis and boards in the open. The food was 'four-man ration packs' prepared by army cooks and much better than Meals Ready to Eat (MRE) or 'rat packs'. Overall conditions were good but a bit rough and ready. I have lived in much worse.

The next deployment was to the Peace Monitoring Group (PMG) in Bougainville which had been established for a reasonable period of time and so had settled into routine comfort. We lived in 11-feet by 11-feet tents with a stretcher, mosquito net and canvas storage for personal belongings. All accommodation, mess, administration and other support were lodged in similar tents. The whole caboose was erected under the roof of a monster-sized ore processing plant that had been used to prepare and export copper from the Panguna mine in the middle of the island. The mine was one of the main catalysts for the civil war between Papua New Guinea and Bougainville and had stopped production as a result of the hostilities. The processing plant at Loloho/Arawa no longer received raw material and so was abandoned and became derelict. Its roof covered the entire ADF hospital, staff accommodation, vehicle storage and logistics. The structure provided excellent additional protection from tropical sun, tropical rain and tropical wind.

The toilets in Bougainville were not up to the high standard of the accommodation. They consisted of pits with sanitary collectors. There were two rows facing each other with hessian sacks hanging down to provide limited privacy. It was not high enough to cover faces. It was an unusual feeling to be sitting on the toilet and looking directly into the eyes of a comrade in arms while we shared bowel motion experiences.

The three deployments to East Timor had successively improving accommodation. The first experience was a bit miserable. The four specialists, (general surgeon, orthopaedic surgeon, anaesthetist, intensive care) were all allocated a single small room that had previously struggled to accommodate three specialists. It was impossible to find room for the stretchers, let alone bags and packs, and so we shifted a wardrobe type of structure out of the room and into the outside passage. This caused absolute outrage among the Sergeants and Corporals who were running the show, mainly because we did it on our own initiative 'without permission'. They individually expressed their indignation by stating that the passageway was an important asset used for other 'essential serv[...] effect was lost when they expressed this independently of each other b[y] differing 'essential services' such as 'cleaners' room', 'storeroom' a[nd ...] room'. This was our first hint that the deployment was not a particularly happy [one] and people were starting to get on each other's nerves. There was obviously no room in our tiny room and it did not seem to be doing any harm in the passage and so we left it there for the duration of the deployment and the system survived intact.

This was the first time that we used 'mozzie domes' instead of mosquito nets. The nets have to be strung up over the camp stretchers with cord and were not always effective because of holes in the netting and a tendency for it to droop and make contact with the body of the sleeping occupant. This provided the mosquitoes with the opportunity to withdraw blood for the rather unequal exchange of malaria or dengue fever. The domes were superior in every way. They consisted of a rubber 'floor' that was continuous with netting held in place by flexible bars like a miniature beach tent. They formed a complete enclosure which was large enough for the stretcher and personal belongings of the occupant. The mozzie domes were squeezed into our little room touching side by side which produced some difficulty getting in and out. I slept on the stretcher for about three or four nights in my usual misery until I realised that the stretcher was no longer essential with the mozzie domes. Stretchers were needed to make netting work but were not essential for the domes. From then on, I slept directly on the concrete floor with a little padding which I found much more comfortable than the stretchers. I never used a stretcher again.

We had deployed in the middle of the wet season. It was stinking hot and over 90% humidity. The rain bucketed down each day but did not provide respite from the heat. It merely increased the humidity and made it more intolerable. The first two weeks were the worst. I did not think that I would ever be comfortable but I had acclimatised within two weeks and then did not notice the heat and humidity. This has happened on each deployment to the tropics, two weeks being convinced that you are not going to survive, followed by tolerance and then followed by something close to the enjoyment of the climate. The room had a door into the passageway but no windows or ventilation. Fortunately, we had been warned of this likelihood before deploying and so had bought standard fans in Darwin that blew out the bad air and let in the good (or perhaps vice versa).

The showers were camp showers consisting of a canvas bag suspended by a rope and pulley. It was necessary to collect a four-gallon drum of water from large, black rubber balloon water storage tanks dotted around the camp and then cart it back to the shower block. The canvas bag was lowered on its pulley, the water poured in and the bag raised again. A nozzle was opened and you had your shower. There were about ten of these in a large room and we all showered together. The water was cold, which was a blessing in the heat and humidity.

The toilets were squats over receptacles. There were sewerage lines on the base but the environmental health team did not know whether they functioned or the final destination of the sewerage and so they could not be used. The unhappy situation in East Timor had been precipitated by a referendum on independence. The large plastic boxes used to collect votes were modified and used as our receptacles for the squats. It was a strange irony that the receptacles for the hopes of the local citizens were receiving much different deposits due to a shortage of resources.

There were all round improvements six months later on my second deployment. Perhaps, it was because this deployment was under RAAF command. Army takes pride in its indestructibility in coping with rough conditions but RAAF is not embarrassed to ensure comfortable living conditions for its members. Hence, the often-repeated saying, 'army lives under the stars, navy steers by the stars, air force chooses its accommodation by the number of stars'. In this case, the step up in luxury was from a claustrophobic, poorly ventilated dog box for the first deployment to sharing two joined tents with three other people. There was more space for baggage and much better ventilation. It seemed luxurious. The mozzie domes also helped to provide a small area of inviolable personal space. The ablution block was even more luxurious with proper water closets for the toilets and hot running water for the showers. The showers were communal and so the area became an enormous, over-heated sauna even worse than the over-heated humidity outside.

The next deployment to East Timor was an even greater step up in luxury. We now had demountable buildings with individual rooms with air conditioning. This unit was under the command of Army Reserve who presumably also identified accommodation with the level of stars. The toilet and shower block retained its communal sauna intimacy.

We had genuine starred accommodation for the urgent deployment following the second Bali bombing. We arrived in C130 aircraft. We gathered the victims from the site of the bombing, assembled them under a shelter at the airport, loaded them onto the aircraft and watched them take off and fly back to Australia. There we were standing on the runway of an Indonesian airport in RAAF uniforms with no equipment, supplies or visible means of support. Effectively, we had invaded a foreign country and the appearance would tend even more in that direction if we wandered around the country in Australian military uniform. A RAAF ambulance had been unloaded from a C130 at the airport and had not been loaded back on for the trip home. It was in the same predicament and I am not sure if it ever made the trip home. I guess it was returned at some stage.

Eventually, we were picked up by transport and taken to a four or five-star tourist hotel. We were taken through the front lobby in a rather scurrying motion so as not to alarm or embarrass the tourists and went straight up to the rooms that had been booked for us. We had taken minimal personal equipment to Bali because it was supposed to be a quick in-and-out operation with minimum baggage of any description. We had our uniforms and not much else. We were instructed to stay in our rooms because we could not venture outside in uniform. Meals were sent up by room service and the hotel provided toiletries.

The next problem was a necessity to change hotels. I never found out why we changed hotels but I presume the first hotel could not accommodate us for more than a night or two. Somehow, we were given appropriate Bali-style shirts and shorts so that we could walk through the hotel lobby disguised as tourists (I doubt that we fooled anybody), into a taxi and off to another four or five-star hotel. We hung around there for another night (or perhaps two) and were then taken to the airport for transport back by Qantas.

This was far and away the most luxurious accommodation that I ever had on deployment but seeing the victims of the bombing was so distressing and the weird circumstances of the departure were so confusing that I never appreciated the comfort of the luxury hotels.

The accommodation in the USAF base in Iraq did not match the commercial hotels in Bali but was super-luxurious by military deployment standards. Because of my rank of Group Captain (equivalent to Colonel), I was accommodated in a demountable hut that had two separate rooms, each with a single bed, desk and primitive cupboard. The two rooms shared an en-suite shower and toilet between them. I was fortunate in that my 'flatmate' was a fellow Australian Army Colonel and we quickly came to a working agreement regarding maintenance and bathroom cleaning. Others in a similar arrangement were not so fortunate in cooperating with their co-inhabitants. Human nature insists that people disagree and fail to collaborate, thus making life that little more miserable. I was able to improve the décor by buying a few cheap mats from the local market. These served the purpose of providing some Middle Eastern colour and enabling me to empty out the bucket loads of sand that inevitably found its way through the door and onto the floor.

The most visible exterior decoration was the stack of sandbags from the ground up to mid-window level. This was to provide protection when the rockets and mortar bombs arrived about three or four times each day. We were warned of the attacks by a siren which usually sounded shortly after the ordnance had hit the ground. We then had to put on our body armour, lie on the ground so that we were below the upper level of the sandbags and cower there in the unlikely event of more bombs arriving.

Ranks of Wing Commander (equivalent to Lieutenant Colonel) and below were much less fortunate. They shared four to a room that was smaller than my single room and they had to walk several hundred metres to the shower and toilet block, usually through the mud, puddles and ice of the Iraqi winter.

The accommodation in Tarin Kowt, Afghanistan, was in a deployable military hospital owned and commanded by the Netherlands defence force. The Netherlands does not have a great need for medical assets that can be deployed within their own country and so they developed something from basic principles. They used shipping-style containers to transport equipment to Tarin Kowt and then transformed them into accommodation on location. They solved the need for protection from bombs and blasts by making the container walls and roof inches thick with armour plating. It was expensive but I presume there was a small saving in sandbags. The interior of the containers lost space because of the thickness of the walls and so they were a tight fit for the four occupants. There were stacked bunks and it was necessary to keep the kit and personal belongings on the bunk where you slept. The containers were arranged together in rows to make a community that was interconnected with covered walkways. Similar communities were accessible by open walkways protected by piles of rocks in wire mesh. This was the NATO method which contrasted with the Americans who used large concrete blocks for the walkways and sandbags for the buildings.

The shower and toilet blocks were all communal and unisexual which was a reflection of the lack of embarrassment of the Dutch with personal exposure. Our ADF female members were understandably a little more coy about this and so were allocated a block for their exclusive use. The facilities were good with warm water for the showers and functioning water closets. There was shortage of water because it was trucked in and so there was also the usual limitation of two minutes showering time. It is amazing what you can achieve during two minutes in a shower.

And so my sleeping conditions have varied from sleeping on a concrete slab with three colleagues in a room about two metres by three metres in East Timor to my own room in a hut with toilet and shower shared with one other person in Iraq. There were tents with open flaps to allow the air to breeze through, an air-conditioned hut, a tent inside a giant shed, a room with en-suite in a damaged hospital and four packed in with double bunks in a confined space divided into tiny compartments. They were not conditions for anyone who craved privacy or was claustrophobic.

Meals were generally of a good standard with well-prepared food in good quantities. There was variation influenced by the country responsible for provisions and meals.

Most of my deployments have been to Australian Defence Force units and the catering section has usually been Australian Army. There was reassuring consistency in types of meals and method of presentation. The breakfasts, lunches and dinners would be recognisable to most Australians. The main variation was on Sundays when the cooks did maintenance chores on the kitchen and then had a well-earned rest for the remainder of the day. Everyone else either lived off 'rat packs', otherwise known as ration packs or Meal Ready to Eat (MRE), or arranged a BBQ amongst themselves using meat and salad supplied by the central stores. MREs were of such a low standard that they were surpassed even by my own cooking. They were small cardboard boxes with a mixture of re-heatable casserole type of food (plus miniature burners for the re-heating), sweets, chocolate, biscuits, cheese, preserved fruit and other non-memorables. The calorie content and food mix were especially calculated to cover one day and you were supplied a number of boxes according to the time that you would be away from mess supplied meals. Four days of MREs was about my limit, both for carrying in my pack and eating for survival.

The USAF base in Balad, Iraq, was huge and the population was equivalent to a reasonable sized regional town in Australia with a population of about 50,000 but with young physically active residents with voracious appetites. There were a number of varying sized messes (American defence force slang was 'chow hall') ranging from monster sized buildings to a small dining room in a back room of the hospital. Most were in the monster category and had an extraordinary range of options for meals. The spectrum was from disgustingly unhealthy lollies and ice cream through to delicious traditional, Asian, Mexican and Mediterranean options. There was every other possibility between. The large serves consumed by hungry American soldiers was impressive. Catering was in the hands of private contractors and they worked from kitchens that matched the size of the halls and the appetites of their many customers. There had been an incident in a mess, elsewhere in Iraq, when an insurgent had managed to dress in the current Iraqi military uniform over the top of a suicide bomb belt and then blown up many unfortunate diners and himself. Our messes always had a US Marine, armed with rifle and clicker, standing guard at the door and all weapons were checked in before entering. One of his duties was to click a little counter in his hand each time someone entered the mess.

Private contractors were also responsible for the mess in Tarin Kowt, Afghanistan, but it was not such a large enterprise because there were defence forces from a number of the NATO countries and they tended to provide their own catering and messes. The ADF Special Forces spent long and exhausting periods of time living dangerously while on patrol and so had ADF cooks who served up good Australian fare, such as BBQs, when they were back on base. Occasionally, the medical team was invited to join them. Otherwise, we dined in the central mess that had a strong Dutch flavour to it and was healthy and enjoyable.

Managing one's own health and physical well-being is a vital responsibility while on deployment. Those who rescue, aid, treat or protect others are of no use to those who need their help if they allow themselves to be damaged in any way. Then the helper becomes one of the victims and adds to the problems of the remaining helpers. Better if they had not arrived on the scene at all.

The precautions start at the pre-deployment training with information on health risks and climate factors such as extreme heat, extreme cold, too much rain, not enough rain, dust storms, jungle and desert. The cliché 'austere environment' understates the risks of being transported to the end of the civilised world. Unfriendly local inhabitants such as spiders, scorpions, snakes, frogs and lizards add interest. Much information is provided on 'vector driven diseases' translated as infections spread by mosquitoes, ticks and other creepy-crawlies. The importance of healthy eating and maintenance of hydration is emphasised.

All of this information seems theoretical at the time of training but its importance becomes apparent in the stark reality of the deployment.

I never deployed to a climate similar to that of my hometown in Sydney. Kigali, Rwanda, was almost on the equator and was hot but tolerable because of its altitude of about 5,000 feet. Papua New Guinea, Bougainville and the Solomon Islands had the hot and humid stickiness of South Pacific tropical islands.

I experienced both the wet and dry seasons of East Timor. Both were hot but the dry season was much more pleasant than the wet when you sweated continually and never dried out because of the humidity. The regular afternoon heavy rains were a relief. Self-preservation required clothing that absorbed and evaporated water plus continually drinking water to maintain hydration. The ADF uniform of heavy trousers, thick cotton T-shirt and woollen socks was surprisingly practical under the circumstances, particularly with the need to cover all parts of the body to protect against mosquito bites.

The Iraq deployment was in the winter of the Northern Hemisphere and was deep inland with extremes of temperatures. Rain, sub-zero temperatures and frost were the first surprising experience with puddles of water turning to ice and then into mud. Spring was arriving towards the end of the deployment and the temperature was rising rapidly into the high thirties centigrade but with zero humidity. Afghanistan provided similar contrast between tropical island and Middle Eastern climate.

I never saw a snake, but I saw a good supply of spiders and scorpions. Guadalcanal, the Solomon Islands, had a huge population of cane toads. They were not harmful but it was unpleasant to feel them crunching underfoot.

Prophylaxis against malaria was essential. The ADF malaria research unit is one of the most advanced in the world and the importance of precautions was always emphasised. Precautions consisted of soaking clothing in insect repellent permethrin, wearing full-length trousers, long-sleeved shirts and hats during the high-risk times of dawn and dusk, sleeping in mozzie domes or netting and taking prophylactic medication. The Environmental Health team protected us by eliminating breeding sites for mosquitoes and regular insecticide spraying of the accommodation. Entire armies have been rendered incapable because of disease outbreaks such as malaria. Battlefield deaths have only outnumbered deaths from natural causes since the development of antibiotics.

There were more cases of malaria and dengue fever than expected when I first deployed to East Timor. There were a number of possible reasons for this such as the reduced level of experience of a large deployment into an area of risk. Another mooted factor was the concentration of the local population into confined areas because of the chaotic situation. This concentration of humans also concentrated the prevalence of the mosquitoes that spread disease and so increased the number of sufferers.

Clean, dry and comfortable clothing helps maintain good health. Most bases provided good laundry services and this also employed the local civilians who were doing it tough because the local commerce and economy had collapsed. The ADF uniform looked as though it would be hot and uncomfortable but in fact was surprisingly cool and comfortable. It also provided good cover against rain, sun and insect bites.

Diet was at the mercy of whoever was tasked to provide meals. Anything was better than the rat packs or MREs and we always looked forward to the arrival of something better. The ADF catering staff always did well with a variety of healthy food under difficult circumstances. Outside contractors meant well and they certainly provided lots of food but not necessarily of the healthiest variety with highly processed carbohydrates getting a bigger role than advisable.

A clean and healthy water supply and safe sewerage disposal are obvious essentials but are not easy to maintain. The environmental health staff's efforts to keep coalition forces in good health were successful but could easily have been disastrously deficient. It was not possible to keep the environment continuously pristine and so there were a few 'outbreaks' along the way such as episodes of food poisoning and dengue fever in East Timor. Overall, their efforts were outstanding. It is one of those unlucky roles that are invisible and unappreciated when successful but are unfairly criticised when there are problems.

Chapter 13
Workplace

The standard of medical amenities and services where I deployed varied according to many factors. The quality of a medical facility can be defined by its physical structure, its equipment, the range of patients who can be treated and its staff.

A major hospital needs an entrance point for urgent and non-urgent patients to arrive for admission. This means an emergency department ready for numbers of casualties, particularly in a warlike environment, and an outpatient department for general practice medicine. It needs to investigate casualties and patients with imaging studies such as X-rays and CT scans and with laboratory testing of specimens such as blood, urine, surgical biopsies and tests for infection. It needs to accommodate patients in wards staffed by competent nurses. It needs operating theatres and recovery rooms post-surgery. It needs an intensive care unit, and high dependency wards for patients too sick for the routine wards, and it needs a physiotherapy department to rehabilitate patients before discharge home.

A deployed military hospital also needs these amenities if it is going to provide full surgical support, but the larger and more complex the hospital, the more staff required and the greater the logistics of deploying the hospital and getting it home again. Therefore, characteristics of the hospital are reduced or eliminated in response to the task of the deployment. The emergency department resources can be reduced, imaging can be limited to X-rays and not CT scans, the numbers of beds in the wards can be reduced, the operating theatre limited to only one room, the intensive care unit and the physiotherapy unit can be removed.

Available equipment determines the level of service of a hospital. Resuscitation equipment, such as ventilators and defibrillators, availability of blood for transfusion and monitoring equipment will determine the quality of care in the emergency department. Similarly, the range of X-ray, scanning equipment and laboratory testing will directly affect patient care. Operating theatre equipment can vary from the minimum required for basic surgery to many sets of instruments specifically matched for a particular operation such as abdominal surgery, orthopaedic surgery, thoracic surgery, neurosurgery and various other specialities, subspecialties and super-specialities. At the other end of the spectrum is a hospital that is 'travelling light' without all sets of instruments. It must compromise with fewer sets that have a greater range of instruments so that the surgeon can improvise with unfamiliar instruments but still get an acceptable end result. This can test the improvisation skills of the surgeon but coping in unsuitable circumstances with inadequate instruments is an essential talent of the military surgeon.

The numbers and qualifications of the staff are determined by the scope of the services provided by the hospital. Sending enough staff with the right training is essential, otherwise the physical structure and equipment are useless. There is no point sending X-ray machines if there is no technician to use it. There is no point including three operating theatres if there are only sufficient staff to run one operating theatre. The more complex the hospital, the more staff are needed and the more staff, the greater the logistic problems such as travel, accommodation, meals, toilet blocks and recreation. More staff are needed to support the increased numbers of hospital workers, which creates a need for more facilities which require increased staff and so on.

The purpose of the deployed health facility is decided by civilian politicians and that means the Australian Federal Government in most ADF deployments. The exceptions are when ADF health personnel are seconded to facilities owned by other countries or organisations such as the UN in Rwanda, Government of USA in Iraq and NATO in Afghanistan.

Once the political decision to provide the health facility has been made, senior uniformed defence force planners decide on the capability of the facility and hence the structures, equipment, accommodation and personnel to be deployed. The capabilities are partly formalised as Role 1 (minimal), Role 2 (good medical care but not surgery) and Role 3 (surgical care included).

Requirements for each Role have been planned long ago but with sufficient flexibility to allow enhancement or downgrading of the different Roles.

A number of factors are considered. Will the health unit only be treating military personnel or will it also be treating local civilians? If the latter, children and pregnant women may be patients and so specialist obstetric and paediatric equipment may be needed. Will the deployment be non-warlike or warlike? Resources will be needed for blast injuries and high-velocity gunshot wounds if it is warlike. How many people will be relying on the deployed health unit? More people mean more sick and injured patients and so a larger facility is needed. This means more staffing and greater logistical problems. Will it be possible to treat and rapidly transfer patients or will it be necessary for them to remain in hospital for a long time? This will influence the number of hospital beds provided and the surgical capability required because the resources needed for immediate 'damage control' surgery are quite different from, those required for second and third operations aiming for final conclusive surgery or reconstructive surgery. What are the resources already existing in the host country? It is often easier to take over an existing hospital than build a temporary transportable hospital. Will the local hospital be large enough for the deployed military hospital? Is there access to transport? Is there an airstrip that will accept aircraft at least as large as a C130? Is there a functioning port that is accessible for decent sized ships? Does the military force such as the ADF have the resources and personnel available for a deployment? Will the deployed health unit be secure and, if not, will other military personnel need to be deployed to provide security? This usually means deployed infantry and so increased logistics made more complicated because of weapons, ammunition and explosives. How urgently is medical support needed? Rapid response deployment of a health facility usually means it goes in with limited resources and then expands as needed. If there is the luxury of available time, planning can ensure that all resources and personnel are concentrated and trained before deployment. What is the likely duration of the deployment? Planning for a health deployment that will be definitely over in about one or two weeks is different from planning for one that is open ended.

The best planning can become irrelevant because of 'mission creep'. The original plan may have been treatment only for military personnel but the decision is made in the host country to treat civilians, including pregnant women and children. The original plan may have been for a precise period of time but the deployment goes past that time and goes on and on.

The health unit in Vanimo, PNG, was deployed urgently and was never going to remain in place for more than two weeks. Planning was different for the health units in East Timor and the Solomon Islands which were intended to remain in place for many years.

The Vanimo deployment was at short notice, for a specific purpose and for a short period of time. Seismographs recorded an earthquake to the east of Papua New Guinea and there were predictions that a tsunami would strike the northeast coast of the country. There was suspicious silence from the endangered area and so a RAAF C130 Hercules flew over the coastline and confirmed the disaster. There was high-level consultation between the governments of Papua New Guinea and Australia and it was decided that Australia would send immediate assistance in medical aid including environmental and public health resources. Responsibility for planning and implementation was delegated to the ADF and down to the senior ADF Health commanders. The Australian Army rapidly deployable surgical team based in south-west Sydney was given the task 24 hours after the tsunami. Fortuitously all members of the team were at a formal dinner in the barracks on the night that the decision was made. Clothes were changed from formal mess kit to Disruptive Pattern Camouflage Uniform (DPCU) also known as 'Cams'. Planning changed from strategic to tactical. The material was unpacked, checked and repacked. Personnel were selected, briefed and equipped. RAAF health units coordinated provision of the ubiquitous C130 and tasked a medical evacuation team to accompany the army surgical team. The two teams concentrated at the RAAF Base and departed with some uncertainty about the final destination. Options were considered in flight and the decision was made for Vanimo because it was known to be unaffected by the tsunami and had a sealed runway capable of accepting C130 aircraft. The planning was *ad hoc* and reactive but was so effective that the teams arrived within 48 hours of the tsunami.

The surgical unit had departed without an orthopaedic surgeon and so I was selected to join them and arrived within another 48 hours. This gave me a first-hand look at a basic field hospital that had been rapidly deployed and was not expected to remain in place for long.

I landed at the Vanimo Airport in a C130 and was immediately taken to the deployment in a vehicle 'borrowed' locally. I left my backpack in the accommodation which was a disused school and immediately went to see the field hospital and get to work treating the multitude of casualties. The casualties with major internal injuries had all died within the first 48 hours before the first C130 arrived. Casualties with limb injuries, such as major wounds and fractures, had survived and hence the need for an orthopaedic surgeon.

First of all, I went to the operating theatre. This was identifiable by the casualties lying on stretchers outside in the open air under the shade of palm trees attended by staff members and friends and relatives. Some were waiting for surgery and some were recovering from surgery. The operating theatre consisted of three 11 foot by 11-foot tents combined together. The first was a combination anaesthetic and recovery area where casualties were anaesthetised before surgery and then resuscitated afterwards. The theatre itself was the combination of two tents. It was crowded, hot and stuffy. Ventilation was helped by keeping flaps open at both ends of the tents. The operating table consisted of a McVickers Frame, lightweight and easily dismantled for transport. The casualties were brought in on a NATO litter (which is a collapsible stretcher) and the litter rested on the frame while the operation was performed. Lights consisted of small industrial lights on stands and hand-held torches for hard-to-see nooks and crannies in the injured body.

Surgeons wore minimal clothing covered by paper gowns because of the extreme heat and humidity. The clothing made little difference to the sweat soaking out from the inside or the blood and body fluids soaking in from the outside. There was no pretence at infection control because it was now four days since the injuries and wounds were already severely infected. Power was provided by a noisy generator close by. Anaesthetic equipment and theatre equipment were just as noisy. Any emergencies that increased the workload meant a second NATO litter was set on trestles so that surgery could be performed simultaneously on a second casualty. It was an overwhelming environment of people, equipment, sweat, blood, noise, heat, smells, discomfort and stress. After surgery, the patients were taken to the combined anaesthetic/recovery zone to wake up and then taken on their stretchers to lie outside under the palm trees until they were conscious enough to go back to the ward.

The ward consisted of a large public building that had been converted to accommodate casualties. I never found out its previous role but I think it may have been part of the school. There were rows of patients on a variety of sleeping options ranging from mats on the floor, stretchers and ordinary beds. There were many friends and relatives available to provide essential help. We certainly did not have enough staff to provide full care and would not have managed without a lot of help from local civilians. Some casualties had no friends and relatives because they had arrived from a distance. Possibly some had lost all of their friends and relatives to the tsunami. This meant more work for the ADF personnel. Local civilians and the local Catholic community provided wonderful assistance and support when patients were discharged.

My admiration of the Catholic Church increased after this deployment, as it did after my deployment to Rwanda. The contrast between their circumstances at this tsunami in Vanimo, PNG, and Saint Peters Cathedral in Vatican City is extreme.

There was not much else to the hospital. There was a minimalist portable X-ray that provided feeble and cloudy films developed with chemicals that were struggling to succeed in the heat and humidity. The pathology testing was basic haematology and biochemistry. There was no microbiology to identify infecting bacteria. Deployed military surgeons must tolerate and adapt to these limitations that are delightfully understated by the euphemism 'austere environment'. It distinguishes the military surgeon from the civilian surgeon who is accustomed to the reassurance of backup resources.

The deployment to the Solomon Islands was to a medical unit supporting Australian Federal Police (AFP) posted following an agreement called RAMSI (Regional Assistance Mission to the Solomon Islands) between the Governments of the Solomon Islands and Australia. Their task was to assist the local security forces to maintain law and order where previously there was anarchy. The ADF was tasked with providing support such as air transport, health facilities, food, environmental protection from infectious diseases, water supply, sewerage disposal, etc. The buildings were erected by civilian contractors. The base was located at Henderson Airport and had been a luxury resort in a previous life but had been badly knocked around during the civil war. The hospital consisted of buildings that were pre-fabricated and could be rapidly erected and demolished. It was quite luxurious for a deployed facility. The wards, operating suite and outpatient facilities were clean, easily maintained and air-conditioned. The exception was the accommodation for the medical staff. We lived in tents with cane toads, mosquitoes and lizards for company. The hospital provided medical care for the healthy AFP and ADF members and so there was not a lot to do.

It was more interesting to go to the much busier but under-staffed local hospital and help with the care of the local civilians. The hospital was well established with good buildings and facilities. The architecture was typical 'tropical hospital' with long corridors servicing wards, offices and allied health services that branched out like ribs from the spine of the corridor. These ribs had doors and windows that could be opened onto expansive verandas. Most of it was not air-conditioned but the clever design made it tolerable in the tropical heat and humidity. Equipment and facilities were equivalent to a public hospital in a reasonably sized country hospital in Australia. They had lost staff during the hostilities but nurses and medical specialists were returning to their homeland and services were getting back to normal.

In truth, the hospital did not need help from the deployed ADF specialists, doctors or nurses. The staff were hard-pressed by the heavy workload but they were accustomed to this and were also knowledgeable about the local diseases, particularly those linked to the tropics and the lifestyle habits of the citizens. Diabetes with all of its complications was endemic.

We in the deployed ADF team were pleased to visit the hospital and get involved with outpatient and in-patient treatment including scrubbing and operating in the theatre suite. Our help was not essential and the visits were mainly professional interaction between hosts and visitors with one learning from the other. The local doctors and nurses were knowledgeable and experienced about the limitations of what they could achieve with less than optimal equipment and patients who could be wilful and uncooperative. This was instructional for ADF doctors and nurses who were spoilt by the luxurious facilities, abundant equipment and high staffing levels in the main centres of Australia.

My experience in Bougainville was similar but different in details. This deployment was also a long-term peacekeeping force following a ten-year civil war, in this case involving Bougainville and Papua New Guinea. The war had resulted in the destruction of all public facilities including the local hospital.

The deployed ADF hospital was the 'heavy' version of the Australian Army field hospital and included an operating theatre, X-ray facilities and high dependency beds in containers. Everything else was in tents and it all sheltered under the huge building constructed of wood frame and iron cladding which was the old factory for initial processing of raw copper from the mine.

The hospital was well established and had good facilities but was a typical field hospital with limited equipment and reliance on the flexibility and resourcefulness of the staff to achieve its mission. It was primarily charged with the healthcare of the ADF personnel and Australian public servants posted to Bougainville. Because the local hospital had been destroyed and there had been no effective health system for ten years, there was a great need for health support for the local population and so we also treated local civilians. The extent of this service depended on the tolerance of the ADF Commanding Officer and the current workload of the hospital.

As a general observation on my deployments, there was variability between Commanding Officers and their indulgence in allowing treatment of civilians in ADF facilities. The stricter variety of CO was often fearful that the hospital would be filled up with civilians and there would be no room for ADF members. This never happened during any of my deployments, even with particularly liberal commanders. The mismatch between medical specialists' desire to be humanitarian and commanders' desire to follow orders and fulfil their mission could sometimes lead to friction between these participants.

At the time of the arrival of the ADF peace monitoring force, the local health system varied between bad, non-existent and shambolic. There were rumours of a total lack of medical care in locations outside the main centre. There appeared to be no medical treatment at all and sick and injured were simply left to live, die or recover according to their fate.

In East Timor, I was posted to the same hospital and the same physical location in my three deployments. We were in a commandeered museum located halfway between the airport and the town centre of Dili. The wards were on two levels of the display area of the museum. I never saw any of the exhibits. I do not know whether they were destroyed or simply stored out of harm's way. The other hospital services were in a combination of tents and expandable containers that were components of the 'heavy' Army deployable field hospital. I could see a little improvement in the facilities each time I deployed but the basic set-up stayed much the same.

The biggest improvement was in the 'infection ward' which, on my first deployment with INTERFET, was a tent for the isolation of patients with malaria, dengue fever and gastrointestinal infection. The deployed hospital was in its infancy at that time and was struggling to get mosquito-carried diseases under control. Insecticide spraying was constant but, even so, the "infection ward" seemed to be a popular habitat for mosquitoes with many of them living comfortably under the canvas layers of the tent. Fortunately, the incidence of transmissible diseases was controlled and the need for a specific ward decreased so that the few cases could be isolated in the general ward on my later deployments.

Why were malaria and dengue fever so prevalent early in the operation? There are a number of theories and, like many medical events, there were most likely a number of factors. Certainly, the time of year, which was the wet season and humid and hot, was a factor. Public health and medical availability had decreased during the mayhem that had occurred just prior to the arrival of INTERFET. Population shift also played a part. East Timor is a largely rural country with most of the people living distant from others. The turmoil had caused the population to shift and concentrate in urban areas and towns and so large numbers of people were squashed into temporary camps and accommodation. This was an ideal situation for the spread of infection by mosquitoes. ADF members were not immune despite the requirement to take prophylactic anti-malarial medication. There was a significant incidence of malaria and dengue fever in the deployed force.

The operating theatre in East Timor had the standard military deployable anaesthetic equipment and surgical trays of instruments. Limited transport and supply mean that not all likely medical events can be covered and so anaesthetists and surgeons needed to be flexible and resourceful when surgical instruments did not match the operation being performed.

The design and buildings of the local hospital in Dili, East Timor, were similar to the hospital in Honiara, Solomon Islands. This was not a coincidence but was an identical solution to similar circumstances. Both were on tropical islands with varying climatic conditions throughout the year. The description of 'wet season' and 'dry season' is an oversimplification. The Australian aborigines who live in the tropical north identify about six or eight different weather patterns that occur cyclically through the year and the tropical islands are the same. The hospitals are always hot and humid and air conditioning is not available but the people are well acclimatised to the heat and find an ambient temperature much below 30°C as uncomfortably cold. Consequently, the public hospital in Dili conformed to the conventional design of a tropical hospital. It was a series of single-story bungalows connected by open passageways that were sheltered from sunshine and rain by flimsy roofing. The bungalows had surrounding verandas for shade and large windows that could be opened wide to allow a cooling breeze to flow through the building. The design worked well and the buildings were comfortable and soothing.

I deployed twice more and there had been a significant improvement to the public hospital each time. The International Committee of the Red Cross (ICRC) provided staff, including some of my civilian colleagues from Australia, and there were volunteers sponsored by bodies such as the Royal Australasian College of Surgeons. The services were eventually contracted to civilian medical providers and specialist staff were employed on short-term contracts. East Timorese doctors and nurses slowly gravitated back to their homeland to resume their careers. The East Timorese health service was gradually approaching normality at the time of my final deployment.

The military hospitals in Balad, Iraq, and Tarin Kowt, Afghanistan, were in active war zones and their purpose was medical support for military personnel engaged in combat. Balad was a US deployment and Tarin Kowt was the Netherlands but both countries had produced similar answers to the question of how to deploy a mobile hospital. Before deploying, the equipment and stores for a unit of the hospital, such as a ward, a physiotherapy department or an operating room, were packed into a container that appeared similar to a conventional shipping container. The size of the hospital determined the number of containers.

The Balad hospital must have been packed in about 30 containers. The containers were transported to their destination and then unpacked. The containers themselves folded out to become shelters. The US defence force used air-conditioned tents that extended out from the containers and then connected with adjacent tents from adjacent containers. The end result was a corridor 'spine' with attached 'ribs' of wards, outpatients, intensive care, physiotherapy, administration and sundry other hospital essential services. There were two spine and rib structures. The operating theatres remained in the folded-out containers and were connected to the rest of the hospital by tents. The structure had been carefully worked out and functioned well. Sandbags were piled two-thirds of the way up the walls and concrete bunkers were scattered around the hospital.

The Tarin Kowt hospital used the same system of packing all equipment in containers that folded out and interconnected with each other. The main difference was that the containers were about 10 cm thick armoured steel and there were no tents. Sandbags and bunkers were not necessary because we sheltered in our armour-plated accommodation. The place was ringed with steel mesh and rock shelters. Tarin Kowt was a smaller hospital without the multitude of resources of Balad such as image scanning, multiple operating theatres, physiotherapy, ICU with ventilators, etc., and so there were fewer containers. It was an asset owned by the Dutch military and was a transportable hospital developed for deployment overseas. The Netherlands is a small and densely populated country which does not need a transportable hospital available for deployment within its own borders. Their defence force would always find a suitable local civilian hospital in the Netherlands, if they were ever required to deploy internally, because there is a major population centre with a hospital within easy reach everywhere in the country.

This contrasts with Australia which is large and sparsely populated outside the main cities. There are large areas with no medical facilities and so a force that is deployed within Australia needs the support of a transportable hospital. All three ADF services have some form of deployable medical facility because an ADF deployment within Australia is likely to find itself a long distance from an established medical facility. Ironically the Dutch military transportable hospital was much better than the ADF transportable hospitals, though much more expensive. The ADF medical team looked at it with a degree of envy. There was an interesting reaction when we were visited by the Australian Chief of Army who immediately sensed the medical team's desire to get something similar. He took one step through the front door and announced that it was "very impressive" but that Australia "did not need anything like this".

The local civilian hospitals were always an interesting contrast with the military hospitals. The public hospital in Kigali, Rwanda, was called Central Hospital Kigali (CHK) and was large but typical 'third world' type of hospital with dirty, crowded wards and a shortage of equipment, resources and especially staff. Doctors and nurses had not been protected during the massacre. It was said that one head of the department was Hutu and he personally killed all other members of the staff because they were Tutsi. Tutsi medical staff who survived the massacre fled the country. Hutu staff may have remained initially but they also ran for their lives when the Tutsi-led Rwandan Patriotic Army came to town to avenge the massacred Tutsi. The end result was that there were few doctors and nurses and some that remained had doubtful or non-existent qualifications. Nursing care for inpatients was usually done by friends or relatives who 'camped' in the hospital next to their dependant. This was essential while in hospital but unfortunately it often continued when the patient went home and remained completely dependent on friends and relatives. It was not unusual for them to continue lying in bed at home and enjoying total care so that they made no attempt to get up and walk but were carried everywhere by their over-zealous carers.

Health professionals from other African countries and the Indian sub-continent were starting to drift in to help but their standard and experience were variable and all of them struggled to cope with the lack of resources for the overextended conditions. Despite all of the problems, there were some impressive individuals amongst these visitors who were accustomed to the medical equivalent of 'flying by the seat of their pants' by making decisions with limited laboratory and radiology resources. They were much more reliant on their history and examination skills than a 'western civilisation' doctor such as myself and they had good judgement as to whether surgical treatment was likely to be a small step forwards or a complete disaster. The ADF surgical team used to visit CHK to provide the benefit of our expertise but I think that I learnt more from them than I taught.

I did regular orthopaedic outpatient clinics at CHK and the clinical material was fascinating. The patients were always polite but always appeared frightened and unhappy, as did the people walking down the street. The whole city appeared to be suffering from mass Post-Traumatic Stress Disorder. There were many sad cases of untreated chronic diseases and deformities. The people were wildly optimistic about the skills of the visiting medical team and were hoping for complete cures of incurable conditions that were beyond any form of treatment. Often a case could be made for major surgery but doing a big operation and then leaving the country and the patient to an unknown future in a doubtful medical system is a recipe for disaster.

My proudest achievement was persuading the local staff to apply hinged cast braces for fractures of the femur. Previous treatment was a choice between a surgically implanted nail, which had a high risk of disastrous infection, or lying in traction for over 12 weeks, which resulted in weakness of muscles and stiffness of joints. The cast brace could get them out of bed and exercising after five weeks without surgery. The key ingredient was the hinged brace made by the visiting prosthetist.

My diary notes of cases in the clinic include deformities due to poliomyelitis (many patients), clubfoot, chronic osteomyelitis with dead bone, tuberculosis of knee, fractured thigh bone healed at an angle of 90°, chronic dislocated knee suffered 12 months previously, malignant bone tumours, machete wound to heel with complete division of Achilles tendon ('punishment' meted out by her boyfriend one year previously), discharging infection of the ankle, severe foot deformities, multiple fractures, etc., etc.

The Australian Army advised us not to communicate or socialise with the RPA (it was just short of an outright order to have nothing to do with them) and similarly the RPA soldiers were forbidden to have anything to do with us. This was ignored by both sides when RPA soldiers had orthopaedic conditions they wanted treated. They then lined up at the clinic dressed as civilians but still recognisable as RPA. They were unrealistically optimistic that a complete cure was going to be achieved by a western doctor and this could make them demanding verging on aggressive. Most of the cases were the complications of untreated gunshot wounds that had occurred about 12 months previously during the civil war.

My record of RPA cases includes non-union fracture tibia after gunshot wound with external fixator still in place after 12 months, upper arm flailing in the breeze because of a gunshot causing loss of 15 centimetres of the arm bone, knee blown to tiny pieces because of a gunshot, etc., etc.

Many of the in-patients were equally distressing: fractured hip waiting four weeks for surgery, fractured shin bone due to gunshot with no prospects of healing without major surgery, broken and dislocated elbow, broken and dislocated wrist, displaced fracture of the neck with total quadriplegia (untreatable in the conditions except for terminal nursing care and so a slow death sentence), multiple trauma, etc., etc.

The civilian staff at CHK and the ADF surgical team took turns to cover acute admissions that presented to CHK. We transferred our patients the short distance from next-door CHK to our own hospital.

The wards in CHK were unhygienic with no available water and anti-septics. Many dirty, bloodstained dressings had not been changed for days. The organisation was haphazard. Frequently, the wrong patient was delivered to the operating suite for a nominated operation. If the correct patient did turn up, frequently the wrong instruments had been set up or the anaesthetist did not arrive. Like many 'third world' hospitals, CHK was the victim of misplaced generosity from more affluent countries. Western hospitals often donate redundant equipment to developing countries but donations from multiple sources result in a mish-mash of incompatibility. CHK had implants for fracture treatment that were weirdly unique and needed specialised equipment to be implanted. The equipment was never donated with the implants. In contrast, other hospitals donated equipment used for implanting fracture fixation metal and joint prostheses but none of the implants. The end result was a mixture of implants that could not be used because there was no essential equipment and equipment and instruments that were useless because there were no implants to go with them.

During my deployment to Balad in Iraq, I never saw a local medical facility nor had contact with one. There must have been something medical in the township of Balad but we had no interaction with them. One of the US Air Force medical officers was tasked to liaise with Iraqi hospitals to accept the transfer of Iraqi citizens being treated by the military hospital. The hospital in the patient's hometown was contacted and most appeared to be in Baghdad. He had stories of crowding, poor hygiene and sterility, lack of staffing and equipment but they were functioning after a fashion. Certainly, the Iraqi patients preferred to stay with us rather than be transferred back to their local hospital. A hospital deployed from overseas can damage the local medical services by replacing them with something that the locals judge as better.

We had a little more contact with the local medical services in Tarin Kowt, Afghanistan. The local hospital informally communicated with our medical services through the hospital administration and sometimes simply by walking to the entrance gates of the base and speaking to the sentry. Telephone communication was possible occasionally and I had a few conversations with staff at the hospital, usually requests to accept trauma patients beyond their capability. A typical accepted patient was a man with a fracture of the femur just below the hip. Ideally, a nail should have been inserted but that type of equipment is not typically available in a military front-line hospital and it is treatment fraught with risks in a low technology health service such as existed in Afghanistan. Wound breakdown, infection, loosening of the metal implant and lack of post-operative supervision are all dangers. The end decision was to apply traction to the limb to keep it at the right length and keep it comfortable. The equipment for that was not available either and so improvised bits of machinery were commandeered to connect to a pin through the shinbone and then other bits were used as weights. The patient was then transferred back to Tarin Kowt hospital.

I learnt much more about Tarin Kowt Hospital when we were visited by their one and only surgeon. I requested the visit to try to get more efficient cooperation between our two hospitals and he was keen to visit so that he could find out who we all were, what we had and whether we had training opportunities for him. He was born and went to school in Afghanistan. His medical and surgical training took place in Pakistan and Kabul. He had been a practising surgeon for three years and was in his mid-thirties. He was knowledgeable despite his on-going education opportunities being limited to reading journals and textbooks. He had no access to the internet or interaction with surgical colleagues such as clinical meetings in the hospital or conferences. I had no opportunity to see the quality of his surgical work.

He described the Tarin Kowt Hospital as a significant entity with the capacity for 53 patients divided into male and female wards but usually with occupancy of about 15 to 20 patients. There was a separate obstetric unit built by the ADF Reconstruction Task Force. There were sufficient staff numbers with five general duties doctors and about 15 qualified nurses, including midwives and nurse-anaesthetist. There were two operating rooms and a High Dependency Unit. Funding was partly public, either from the central government or provincial government, and partly from a non-government organisation (NGO).

At the time of his visit, he was waiting for approval and finance to spend a week in Kabul for further training. We heard no more of him and later learnt that he never returned from Kabul.

Few female patients were referred from the local health systems in either Iraq or Afghanistan. This was partly because of the social and cultural isolation of women that prevented them from mixing with the perceived evil of the combined male and female staff at our facility and partly because the men were the ones out and about while women were confined to their home and much less likely to be injured.

In Bougainville, the local medical clinic was a combination of wanton destruction of resources and a tribute to local resourcefulness. There had been a high-quality hospital with good buildings and equipment before the civil war but it was a victim of the anarchy during a war that lasted ten years until the truce and entrance of the UN-backed ADF Peace Monitoring Group. The rumour was that both sides had wanted to preserve the hospital but an out-of-control rebel decided to burn down the entire structure against the orders of his superiors who wanted to keep it for their own advantage. Apparently, he was summarily executed. All that was left was a pile of ash and a number of burnt out modern ambulances that had been gifted by other countries.

The local nurses had commandeered a disused and rather derelict motel and had converted it to a combined hospital and clinic. A lot of the patients were accommodated on a first floor accessible only by a narrow staircase that made access and transfer of patients difficult. All education and training had stopped for the ten years since the civil war and so the nurses covered a spectrum from fully trained, to partially trained and all the way down to untrained. All were keen to commence or resume their training and this was a big part of our role in Bougainville. Their combination of cheerful enthusiasm and thirst for knowledge was inspiring.

There were many rumours of brutal solutions for medical problems for the ten years of the civil war before the truce, such as victims with fractures of the lower limb being dragged into the jungle to die and high mortality rates during childbirth due to lack of obstetric services. We could never establish the truth or otherwise of these rumours.

I deployed to Dili in East Timor three times and the local public hospital was different in character each time, reflecting the slow progress of a country getting back onto its feet.

The first deployment occurred a few months after the country had been torn apart by the political upheaval of gaining independence from Indonesia. Militia who did not want the change adopted their warped solution of burning the city using petrol tankers to hose petrol into buildings and setting them alight. I can recall street after street of burnt buildings. The local public hospital was not completely immune to the devastation but had not been torched into oblivion.

We visited the hospital on the first day of our deployment to Dili. It was being used by the International Committee of Red Cross (ICRC). There were competent international doctors and nurses working in a hospital with an ideal layout for the tropics. The wards were single level with wide verandas and large windows that could open to allow a relieving breeze. Operating theatres, clinics and allied health units were similar. All were connected by external corridors that were open except for shelters overhead.

We did not have a lot of contact with them on this first deployment. We borrowed instruments, such as obstetric forceps, at various times and our staff visited to provide help occasionally. Security was tight because of the dangers from an active and hostile militia outside our wire. Opportunities to move about were severely restricted and we were on call 24 hours 7 days a week in case of injuries to the troops who were risking their necks outside.

There were fewer restrictions on my next deployment six months later and we were allowed to walk around town, though only in company with other ADF members and with loaded rifles. The local hospital was still being managed by ICRC (and was now called the ICRC Hospital) and our contact was more regular. I did orthopaedic clinics where I saw the usual wide range of conditions such as untreated dislocation of the elbow, gunshot wound to arm, born with extra toe, severe deformities at birth and so on. The ICRC orthopaedic surgeon was a colleague from Australia and so it was possible to assist him with some of the more complex cases. The hospital was clean, well-staffed, equipped and managed. We were not allowed to wear our uniform in the hospital because it distressed the East Timorese staff, particularly those who were working before independence. It was said that our uniforms reminded them of the times that soldiers used to come into the hospital and shoot patients.

One year later, on my third deployment, ICRC Hospital had changed its name to Dili General Hospital. It was managed by the local health system but was still dependent on foreign doctors, some of whom were unpaid volunteers and some were on paid contracts. The types of cases treated by the hospital pointed to lawlessness and risk of disintegration of society. There were violent crimes such as stabbings and there were ugly cases of child-rape.

We shared an emergency call with Dili General Hospital and we met the staff socially in restaurants and at mealtime clinical meetings in their hospital. It had become much like the normal relationship between two hospitals in one city, to the extent that we argued and disputed about the transfer of patients between the hospitals.

Chapter 14
Military Hardware and Weapons

It is interesting to see the machinery and technology required for a military deployment. The deployment can be as large as a moderate-sized regional town and as small as a school camping outing. The average was equivalent to a village of several thousand people, all of whom needed transport, feeding, accommodation, security, hygiene and their tools of trade set up in a vacant field with no infrastructure.

Transport vehicles were the common denominator in all deployments. There were light transporters for small numbers of commuters. Toyota Land Cruisers and Hiluxes were ubiquitous in all defence forces. I cannot recall any deployment when I was not shifted around in a Land Cruiser or Hilux at some time. Even insurgents and terrorist organisations liked Hiluxes. They fitted them with 50cal machine guns in the tray and they became a formidable rapidly mobile attack force.

My first sighting of the High Mobility Multipurpose Wheeled Vehicle (HMMWV), famous as the American Humvee, was in Iraq and they were everywhere. The designation 'multipurpose' was most appropriate as they were used for everything such as personnel transport, personal staff cars for the privileged, tow trucks, weapon carriers such as machine guns and rocket-propelled grenades, reconnaissance vehicles, mobile communication stations, ration and supply carriers for patrolling troops, ambulances and just about anything else imaginable. There were many modifications for specific purposes, resulting in a multiple of shapes and attachments. The medical services used them as rapidly deployable ambulances for immediate treatment and rescue of battlefield casualties. They were frequent visitors to our medical unit.

There were two distinctly different looking Humvees. The first ones to arrive in Iraq lacked effective armour plating and had been particularly susceptible to roadside bombs and high-velocity rifle attacks. These had been rapidly fitted with improvised plating that looked ugly and amateurish but was apparently effective. The later ones came equipped with armour and looked much better, but were still vulnerable to a large mine or bomb in the road, usually resulting in wounded or killed occupants.

The vulnerability of the Humvee to mines and IEDs was the motivation for the ADF to develop the Bushmaster multi-purpose armoured personnel carrier with its bomb-resistant design features. It has thick armour plating that forms a sealed, blast-protected compartment separate from appendages such as wheels and transmission. The undertray is V-shaped to deflect any blast. This protects the occupants but sacrifices the appendages that are blown off from the main structure.

My deployment to Afghanistan was my first opportunity to see these remarkable vehicles in action and confirm that they did their task well.

Bigger transporters were Mack trucks and Mercedes-Benz Unimogs. They had plenty to do and so there were plenty of them. They transported large amounts of cargo and large numbers of people as required.

The army was still using the tracked Armoured Personnel Carrier (APC) when I was in Rwanda and this was upgraded to the eight big-wheeled Australian Light Armoured Vehicle (ASLAV) for later deployments. Australia did not deploy tanks but there was a healthy selection to choose from, courtesy of the other contributing countries.

In the Middle East, many diverse vehicles were regularly assembled in the early hours of the morning to depart either on patrol or transporter convoy shortly before dawn. Each transporter was occupied by a driver and several heavily armed guards in armour. Even more heavily armed and manned Humvees were placed between each of the transporters. The event was an assault on the senses. It appeared as if it had been staged by a film director who had lost all restraint in an overblown action production. It was an awesome image of enormous desert-coloured vehicles, soldiers who appeared mechanical and de-humanised because of their body armour, helmets and bristling weapons of various length and calibre. There was soupy mist, exhaust smoke, shouting soldiers, large diesel engines, moving machinery and dust, lots and lots of red dust. Humans and machines would appear out of the gloom to get into position. The humans in body armour, were arrayed with equipment and weapons and looked as machine-like as the machines themselves. The imaging was an ethereal mixture of prehistoric monsters in a movie set such as *Mad Max* or *Star Wars* but coloured in monochrome sepia.

The tropical jungle deployments had equivalent vehicles but on a smaller scale proportional to the smaller scale of the deployments. Unimogs, Land Cruisers and Land Rovers were more numerous than Humvees and enormous transporters. The bright sunshine and clear air removed the otherworldly aspects except when tropical rainstorms made everything seem like rocks in a gigantic waterfall lit up by bolts of lightning.

A common denominator in all deployment was the need for static equipment to provide basic services such as power, water, sewerage and transport. Deployments were rarely plugged into established civilian services and so needed mobile power generators to function. These varied in size and power but none was small, none was quiet and they were usually deployed in numbers. They produced the constant background noise of multiple diesel motors. Eventually, the senses became numb to the constant noise much the same as acclimatisation to tropical heat.

Water was transported in and waste products were transported out in large containers and vehicles. The water was stored in huge rubber bladders interconnected with piping. The effluent was stored in something similar and was pumped out for removal by transporters. The system was well organised and efficient but highly visible.

Deployments were located close to airfields because air transport was vital. This was the mother lode for dedicated plane watchers and a forced enjoyment for those who are not. I personally enjoyed the air movements coming and going. The ubiquitous Hercules C130 figured prominently but it never became boring to look at its distinctive silhouette. I recall them as companions on every deployment. They were at their most dramatic on the dusty and unsealed airstrip at Tarin Kowt. Each landing and take-off was dramatized by huge clouds of dust. It only became a problem after rain when the strip turned to mud or during a sandstorm when all visibility was lost and flights were cancelled.

One-step down was the Caribou DHC-4 that had capability somewhere between the Hercules and a helicopter. It had wide wings and old-fashioned piston engines but it could land and take off from a rugby ground and could be repaired by a bush mechanic. They were remarkably practical and versatile for tactical flights, even though they were as slow as a wet week and struggled with a headwind. I had several 'joyrides' in a Caribou in East Timor and the Solomon Islands. One particularly enjoyable outing occurred in the Solomons when we visited an outlying island for AFP police transfers, health checks and political support.

Working up the hierarchy in cargo aircraft, the next steps are the Starlifter C141, the Globemaster C17 and the Galaxy C5. There were many of these in Balad, Iraq, and quite a number in Tarin Kowt plus unusual NATO aircraft. One "authority" told me an interesting statistic. He stated that the size of a load of a Caribou can fit into the fuel tanks of a Hercules, a load of a Hercules can fit into the fuel tanks of a Starlifter and a load of a Starlifter can fit into the fuel tanks of a Galaxy. I have never been able to confirm this but I include it as an example of the wonderful stories and rumours that circulate on a military deployment.

Much more exciting were the fighters that flew out of Balad in Iraq. This was my only deployment that featured fighter aircraft and they were dramatic. The USAF maintained round the clock fighter patrols from aircraft carriers in the Mediterranean and the Persian Gulf and land-based F16 Fighting Falcons from Balad. The F16s in Balad had the early morning stint and so they took off at about 5 am each morning. Like all aircraft in the area, they were regularly 'locked on' by the radar aiming systems of the insurgent's surface to air missiles and so they were required to reach operational altitude as soon as possible to avoid being targets of the missiles. They took off from Balad vertically like skyrockets under full power and with afterburners working overtime. The sight and sound were awe-inspiring. Their return home was much quieter.

Helicopters figured prominently in all deployments though were not always visible. I cannot recollect seeing helicopters in Rwanda, probably because we were based a distance from the airfield. There were New Zealand defence forces UH1 Iroquois ('Hueys') in Bougainville, a reliable 'utility helicopter' notable for its service in the Vietnam War. The NZ Hueys were twin engine. I asked one of the NZ pilots whether it was reassuring to have the twin engines because there was another engine in reserve if the other failed. His answer was not so reassuring. He said that the aircraft needed both engines and was not able to fly with only one of the engines, which were much less powerful than the customary single engine. He said the result of twin engines was to double the chance of an engine failure. The only benefit was that, if one of the engines was functioning, a single engine was able to provide a safer 'uncontrolled landing' which is helicopter jargon for a crash.

Black Hawk UH60s had become the standard workhorse helicopter for the ADF by the time of East Timor and they worked hard in many different roles. RAN Sea King helicopters were also used until they were grounded after a tragic accident that resulted in a number of casualties including ADF health personnel. The tragedy brought the dangers of military deployments into sharp perspective. The RAAF does not own any helicopters but needs them for search and rescue of aircrew after accidents and so they used private civilian contractors. In East Timor, I had an exciting 'joy ride' with a French Puma helicopter used by a Canadian company that had the rescue contract with the UN and was flown by an ex-RAAF pilot.

The most dramatic helicopter was a Russian monster used for heavy lifting in East Timor. It was owned and deployed by a South American company but was flown by Russian military aircrew who wore civilian clothes and pretended that they were civilians. (Not everything makes sense or is as it appears on military deployments.) The helicopter had enormous rotors that drooped when it was at rest to the extent that they almost touched the ground. It was said that its payload was the same as a C130.

All shapes and sizes of US defence force helicopters were well represented in Balad, Iraq. I could not identify several varieties and am still uncertain what they were. An example of the detail differences is the distinction between the CH-47 Chinook and the CH-46 Sea Knights used by the US Navy for aero-medical evacuation of US Marines. They look similar because they both have twin rotors but the CH-46 is a bit smaller. The other differences need more observation such as three wheels on the landing gear on the CH-46 instead of four and internal engines in contrast to the external engines of the Chinooks. There were a lot of US Army Chinooks in Balad but apparently only a small percentage of the total of between 500 and 1,000 in the entire US defence force. Black Hawks were everywhere and were used for everything. They were the Humvee of the air. The US had more Black Hawks dedicated to aero-medical evacuation in Balad than the total number of Black Hawks in the ADF. The size of the US defence force is gigantic and yet it all seems to work and is remarkably flexible. The aggressive and sinister appearing Apache AH-64 attack helicopters also had a presence in Balad but were not as abundant as the Black Hawks. They intermittently appeared and disappeared on their secretive missions.

Balad was a US base and so the aircraft were predominantly products of the USA. Tarin Kowt was a NATO base occupied by units from a variety of defence forces, all of which contributed to a smorgasbord of interesting helicopters. The Netherland base was visited by aircraft such as Chinooks. Dutch Army Apaches were also on the scene and were designated AH-64D for Dutch. The US also had a base at Tarin Kowt but it was prudently separate from the NATO structure so that they could retain their own command and control. They also contributed to the Apache population. The French had attack helicopters that I never fully identified but I think that they were Eurocopter Tiger EC-665.

The first pilotless aircraft for military use were built and used late in World War I. There has been steady evolution and deployment of drones ever since but recent progress has been exponential and they are now everywhere. My first experience of drones was in the Middle East deployments to Iraq and Afghanistan. I have no idea whether or not they figured on my previous deployments.

Balad was the US base for Predator drones or UAVs (Unmanned Aerial Vehicle) which is the more correct term for such a large machine. We were allowed to inspect one when taken on a tour of the base. It was about a quarter of the size of a glider and built along the same lines with long wings. It was powered by a small, turbocharged piston engine mounted in the rear and was dripping with hi-tech electronic gear, particularly in its top-secret bulbous nose. There were two 'pilot' seats in the hangar which were luxurious lounge chairs surrounded by controls the same as found in the cockpit of a conventional aircraft. The 'pilots' in Balad were only involved in the UAVs take-off and landing. Immediately after take-off, control was handed over to operators in USAF Base Nellis, close to Las Vegas USA, who piloted the craft for its mission because they had the highly sophisticated electronic surveillance equipment. The distance caused a lag in communications that prevented them from controlling take-off and landing and so it was done on base in Balad. If Nellis lost contact, the Predator was programmed to return to Balad and circuit the base continuously until the local pilots landed it.

The Predator had been fitted with two Hellfire missiles but its main task was surveillance, information gathering and laser sighting for bombers, rather than using its own weapons. It was expected that the next generation will be more heavily armed. We were shown interesting video footage of insurgents hiding weapons, firing mortars, setting IEDs and travelling in armed Toyota Hiluxes. One record showed insurgents struck by a Hellfire missile from the Predator as they were setting an IED. The survivors ran a short distance and then could be seen moving in circles in some confusion. They would not have seen or heard the Predator but would only have been aware of a sudden explosion that came from nowhere. Their reaction suggested that they assumed that the explosion was an accidental detonation of their own bomb.

There were similar devices in Tarin Kowt, Afghanistan, but they were much smaller and could be truly called drones rather than UAVs. Watching them depart and return was an entertainment in it itself. The Dutch drones were about the size of a pelican and were rocket launched from a sloping rail. They returned by flying back to base, the engine was stopped and they then descended under a parachute. The ADF drones were about eagle size and could be launched by hand and the landing could be controlled. The electronics had advanced to the stage that the information obtained was comparable to the much larger Predator. The sophistication is continually improving and there are now drones that look like mosquitoes and are the same size.

Also of interest were the remote-controlled robots being developed to disarm or explode IEDs and other booby-traps. They were still experimental and there were several varieties with differing capabilities. The general principle was that they could be guided to the bomb, transmit images for inspection of the device and then disarm it (unlikely), make it explode and sacrifice the robot (most likely) or pick it up and transport it somewhere safer. Fortunately, I only saw them being used in a trial and never 'in anger'.

The US military has also been experimenting with robots providing medical care for casualties but this remained in the 'mysterious rumours' basket during my deployment to the Middle East.

We were taken on a Passport Tour of Balad arranged so that personnel on base could see what everyone else was doing. We saw the Joint Defence Operation Centre (JDOC) that was a huge surveillance headquarters filled with 'spooks' watching TV monitors providing images from the various cameras located many kilometres away from the base. They were the first line of defence against all of the mortar and rocket attacks. They had a vision of the weapons being fired and so could warn of the incoming ordnance before it arrived and could also return fire.

We got a closer look at the vehicles and equipment used for escorting convoys, including US$20,000 laser sights for rifles. We were introduced to the USAF airfield defenders who constantly patrolled several kilometres outside the perimeter in heavily armed Humvees. Their weapons included light machine guns, heavy machine guns, 50cals, RPGs and shoulder-held, single-use rocket launchers (US$600,000 a time). Four Humvees patrolled together with sophisticated communication equipment including cameras transmitting to JDOC.

We were allowed to crawl over F16 Fighting Falcons and look at their support equipment.

We were shown weapons captured from insurgents that covered the full spectrum from sophisticated to homemade and agricultural. This was further amplified by an intelligence officer who stated that some insurgents were complete amateurs who never fused their bombs or rockets and so they never exploded. Others were professional and probably ex-military from Saddam Hussein's forces. They showed video images of one group driving up in a Hilux, rapidly firing off four mortar bombs, packing their equipment and driving off before the return fire had a chance to arrive. All of their bombs exploded on the base. There were stories of insurgents using ice to weigh down the trigger mechanism of the mortars so that they fired when the ice melted and after the insurgent had vacated the vicinity. Civilians such as farmers were paid a few dollars to fire the mortars so that they were the ones at risk and not the insurgents.

Chapter 15
Recreation on Base

All work and no play makes Jack a dull boy or, translating this into the practicalities of a deployment, causes physical deterioration and psychological stress for defence force personnel in a warlike zone. Providing time for recreation and using it positively was given importance on all of my deployments.

The most interesting and enjoyable physical training in Rwanda was the 'truck run'. Volunteering participants were loaded into a Unimog truck and taken five or six kilometres out of Kigali. We were then unloaded and ran back to base. Security was doubtful, and so there were armed guards in the truck and it was compulsory for the group to stay together. Faster runners doubled back to the group when they got too far ahead and slow runners were put back into the truck if they dropped behind. This, combined with the adjutant constantly yelling at everyone, put on a lot of pressure to keep up and I found it hard going for the first few times, particularly because I had not yet acclimatised to the heat and the altitude of 5,000 feet, but I always avoided the truck.

The runs occurred about twice each week and provided a good opportunity to see the countryside and people. There was lush farmland and many people going to work and carrying loads. The women were colourfully dressed and almost all were carrying loads on their heads such as wood, eggs, baskets of vegetables, luggage, live chickens, household equipment and anything else that comes to mind. Men were riding motorbikes and bicycles with larger loads but the same type of goods. They also used motorbikes for family transport and it was not unusual for four, five or six family members to be on board. There were fewer cars than motorbikes. The driving was a bit wild and the pedestrians were careless. Inevitably, we were witness to a fatal accident on one of the runs when a child was run over by a car.

A variation on the theme was the 10 km Kigali 'City to Surf' fun run which was questionable 'city' and certainly not 'surf'. I am not sure who organised it but it was enthusiastically supported by the defence forces of all nations and some civilians. We were driven by truck to the start, wherever that was, and we ran to the Kigali Sports Centre. Many of the ADF medical team participated and there were the expected high-level competitors such as the ADF Infantry Company, the Indian soldiers, Ghurkhas, various small contingents and, most pleasingly, the Rwandan Patriotic Army. The gun went off at 0600 and the RPA and the Ghurkhas went off like hares. I was good for 6.5 km but strained my calf and did a walk/run until the finish. It was won by a Ghurkha who looked as tough as nails. Second place went to a Brit civilian from UNICEF who was ex-British Army and third place went to an RPA soldier. Generally, the RPA ran as a group in the leading bunch and were escorted by a carload of supporters yelling encouragement to them (or so I was told because I was nowhere near the leading group to personally observe). We were supposed to have a BBQ, touch football and a swim when we finished at the Kigali Sports Centre but the RPA changed their mind and would not allow it. We all travelled back to the ADF HQ in trucks and had a BBQ of sausages, fried eggs, bacon and tomatoes for breakfast, thus negating any health benefits of the run.

In Rwanda, we were also allowed to leave the base and go into town as long as we carried loaded rifles. Small groups of two or three of us jogged around carrying a rifle weighing several kilograms which added to the quality of the exercise if not the aesthetics.

We also had social outings in Rwanda. The highlight was a trip to the Canadian contingent's mess to watch New Zealand and England play in the Rugby World Cup semi-final. We arrived after a bumpy ride in a 4wd ambulance with many interesting sights such as wrecked Toyota Land Cruisers with UN markings on the doors scattered around and similar cars being driven by likely looking villains with the UN markings still visible through inadequate paint-overs.

The Canadian Mess was an amazing scene. It was densely filled with cigarette smoke. All four walls were covered with slogans, varieties of T-shirts and sundry weird souvenirs. The customers appeared to be degenerate NGO workers, deadbeats, hangers-on, Maoris and their wives and fanatical England supporters. Many were inebriated, yelling, drinking, smoking and otherwise supporting their team in the sport of the gods which is 'meant for gentlemen but played by cads'. The scene reminded me of the over-cooked and over-acted movie scenes from *Star Wars*, *Raiders of the Lost Ark*, *MASH* and *Apocalypse Now*. I drank Kenyan and Ugandan beer which was pale, strong and suited to the occasion. As far as the game was concerned, Jonah Lomu was at his peak and NZ won comfortably.

We were guests of the UN Medical CO after the game in his accommodation at the "Belgian Village" that had been built to accommodate Sabena airlines staff during the good times. It was a little oasis of appealing bungalows, attractive gardens and a swimming pool. We had pre-dinner wine and beer and then went for dinner in the club or restaurant in the village.

Another notable social event in Kigali was a meal at the Hotel des Milles Collines that won fame in a movie as the '*Hotel Rwanda*'. The hotel was large and luxurious with carpets, large swimming pool, beautifully kept gardens, well-dressed waiters and attendants. We presented in uniform, laid our rifles at the end of the table and enjoyed a good meal but without alcohol because the rifles were loaded.

Otherwise, personal recreation consisted of the usual activities of jogging around the base, exercising in the improvised gym, reading and writing letters. This was my first experience of having limited reading material that is consumed quite quickly. After this, I developed the habit of taking a few books that were relatively small but took a long time to read. Shakespeare's plays are particularly suitable.

There was no time for recreation during the tsunami deployment to Vanimo except for the occasional short run in the evening. Otherwise, the days were taken up with hard work in difficult circumstances and the nights were taken up with recovering. We had two or three days in the end when we could swim at the beautiful local beach that had been tempting us for the duration of the deployment.

Bougainville was a bit the opposite with a lot of downtime but difficulty finding good areas to relax. The beach and sea looked beautiful but the environmental health people had tested the water and found that it was contaminated with heavy metals and other poisons from the adjacent factory that processed products from the mine and so we were unable to swim in it. There was a small remote cove close to the base that was classed as safe but it involved a scramble down a small cliff onto a platform and then a bit of a wallow in a confined space of water. Getting out again was more vigorous exercise than the swimming. Alternatively, there were two kayaks on base that allowed some paddling when the surf was safe. There was compulsory PT and we also organised cricket and volleyball matches.

The three deployments to East Timor had increasing levels of freedom that reflected the improving situation in the country with the passage of time.

We were substantially confined to base on the first INTERFET deployment and exercises consisted of laps of a 420-metre circuit around the base and using the improvised gym. It was compulsory to always carry our loaded rifle and so it was necessary to carry it while running and it had to be kept in sight while exercising in the gym. I ran about six or seven laps each morning and then worked out in the makeshift gym with exercise bike and homemade weight-lifting equipment.

We scarcely moved off base with INTERFET but we were visited by Australian entertainers such as Kylie Minogue, John Farnham, James Blundell and 'Doc' Neeson just before Christmas. Someone had to stay available at the hospital and so we tossed a coin and I lost and had to stay behind. The performances got rave reviews from those who attended and it was a wonderful gesture by the entertainers. I understand that 'Doc' Neeson was the instigator and organiser and his efforts were hugely appreciated because of the quality of the performances and the support from homeland Australia.

The situation had stabilised by the time of my second deployment to East Timor and security had improved sufficiently to allow more freedom of movement and so more recreational activity. The deployment was now under the overall command of the UN and the CO of the hospital was RAAF. This combination also allowed more latitude and there was encouragement to get off base and exercise. An afternoon walk at about 4 pm had become a regular routine. This consisted of a seven to eight-kilometre walk through the local villages to the airport, around the perimeter road and back through the villages. It took about one hour and was therapeutic, both physically and psychologically. As a variation, we occasionally walked up a goat track to the top of a steep hill that overlooked Dili at about 4 am to watch the sunrise. There were 'truck runs' similar to those in Rwanda several times each week and the gym with homemade weight equipment still existed.

A pleasant diversion was Sunday afternoon's Hash House Harriers which had started because of the enthusiasm and persistence of some repeat deploying ADF members and civilian contractors who had been in the country for a long time. The format had commenced in Malaya in 1938. A 'hare' sets the course with hazards and false trails and the followers run as hard and as far as they choose. This was then followed by a BBQ designed to undo all the good work of the exercise. The Hash House Harriers in Dili followed the same format and provided vision of interesting and seldom visited parts of the city.

Commerce was getting back onto its feet in Dili. Most of the buildings had been burnt down during the riots and insurrections that occurred at the time of independence but a few had opened as cafés and restaurants with candid names such as 'The Burnt House'.

The recreation opportunities were much the same in my third deployment to East Timor with regular walks and runs. We were allowed the occasional game of tennis in the neighbouring police barracks. The town was still recovering with increasing facilities and we were able to dine in some of the larger hotels that were deemed suitable for Alexander Downer, Minister for Foreign Affairs, and so were certainly suitable for us.

My next deployment was to Honiara in the Solomon Islands. The workload was not particularly heavy and so outside distraction was encouraged by those in charge. The location of the base in a former recreational and holiday resort made this easier, even though the resort had been severely knocked around during the civil war. There were the usual early morning runs and gym exercises. There was also compulsory Physical Training (PT). Movement off base was much less restricted than on other deployments and so we enjoyed outside activities such as bike riding, tennis on the run-down court in the run-down resort and golf at the local club. I am not a good golfer and I provided further confirmation of this melancholy fact. The most enjoyable aspect was hiring some teenaged schoolboys as caddies. They appreciated the payment they received and they were amusing in their derisive comments about our golfing ability. Their superior attitude was justified because we played several holes with them and they were remarkably talented. We checked the club ladder afterwards and the young lads were playing off handicaps of five or less.

The 'social and entertainment committee' had also arranged alternative entertainment such as trivia nights, competitions on unnatural methods of breaking eggs and time and motion exercises with the local cane toads that reduced their population. We had regular film nights, as was the case on all deployments.

The USAF Base in Balad, Iraq, was equivalent to a town that had been transplanted from conservative USA into one of Saddam Hussein's military academies. It is essential that US servicemen have the comforts of home. Facilities included a full-sized cinema, huge gymnasiums with all modern equipment available, extensively stocked PBX store for electronic equipment and all other necessities, bicycles for sale, tennis and volleyball courts, full-sized swimming pool, shopping mall with fast food outlets, bus service, internet cafés, inside and outside recreational lounges and an all-pervasive loudspeaker communication system that could be heard all over the base. There was regular live entertainment and church services depending on whether you served God or Mammon, though it appeared most US defence force members served both.

All of this created an agreeable habitat but did not quite match my experience of mid-sized towns in the USA. There was a constant coat of fine red dust or mud depending on the weather. There was smoke and haze from the constantly burning rubbish dump. There was the constant sound of helicopters, aircraft, gunshots from the training range and explosions due to bomb disposal and unwanted 'incoming ordnance'. The films in the cinema were frequently interrupted because an NCO would arrive and call out for his unit to report for duty immediately, whereupon about half of the audience would get up and leave. The bicycle rides were good initially but I became more inhibited when told about insurgents taking pot-shots at cyclists if they wandered too close to the perimeter. Similarly, the bullet holes visible in the bodywork of the buses were discouraging. The electronic equipment and internet cafés were appreciated but lost some relevance because of the frequency and duration of internet blackouts for security purposes. We had no internet or email access for the last four weeks of the deployment. The loudspeaker communication was mainly along the lines of orders to head for the shelters because of more 'incoming ordnance' or calling for volunteers to donate blood because the number of casualties had increased demand.

The NATO Base in Tarin Kowt, Afghanistan, was a composite of various units from various nations that worked together but tended to live and relax separately and so there were not the large-scale facilities found in Balad. My main physical exercise was early morning runs around the perimeter of the base followed by exercises in the gymnasium. We also had an informal five-man soccer match with the Dutch who would have comprehensively massacred us if we had not positioned our 201cm tall anaesthetist in front of goal on a chair so that he obliterated all access to the goal and made scoring almost impossible. The Dutch were not happy about it because it reduced their winning margin from total massacre to only a massacre. My mental exercise was reading, research for scientific papers and floundering attempts to learn the French language. There was intermittent internet availability depending on circumstances such as security, current combat action or recent casualties when the powers above shut down access to prevent information leaking off base.

Chapter 16
Exploring off Base

My deployments have taken me to different people and cultures in exotic locations and ancient civilisations. The desire to get out and look around was strong but the nature of a military deployment is that your commitments on base restrict sightseeing and tourism. Call work as an orthopaedic surgeon tended to be twenty-four hours every day and travel outside the base perimeter was sometimes too dangerous.

The deployment to Vanimo, PNG, for the tsunami provided the closest contact with the local culture because of the humanitarian nature of the task. We had close contact with local citizens who expressed friendship in many ways in gratitude to the assistance we were providing. The lasting impression is of colourful tropical clothing and huge smiles. They offered all possible help and the local Catholic Church was a shining light in a grim situation. Some of us flew from Vanimo to Wewak in the last few days of the deployment and performed a few surgical operations at the local hospital. The drive from Wewak Airport to the hospital was through lush green jungle along a dirt track, dodging potholes like a slalom course. We stood on the tray of the pick-up truck, clutching the roof of the cab while we watched another pick-up truck approaching on a collision course from the opposite direction. The drivers knew what they were doing because they coordinated their zigzag course as we passed.

Groups from the various 'Wantoks' of the area presented a 'Sing Sing' the day before we returned to Australia. 'Wantok' is pidgin English for a close community that is bound together by one dialect of language and so the Sing Sing represented the local communities that were expressing their gratitude for our assistance. The performances were individually different but all featured colourful costumes and much music and dancing. It was fascinating and spectacular. The musical skills with simple instruments combined with singing were particularly enjoyable and demonstrated the inborn music culture of the local civilisation. We were required to reciprocate and so sang some Australian standards such as *'A Kookaburra sat in an Old Gum Tree'*. Our kookaburra laughs were well received but I am sure our off-key singing contrasted badly with the harmony of the local performers. The New Zealand contingent's contribution was to take off their shirts and do the haka accompanied by whoops and wolf whistles by the local women.

Freedom to travel in East Timor increased with the improved security of each successive deployment.

The first deployment was restricted because of continuing danger from insurgency and impressions were limited to the trip to and from the airport and the occasional trip to provide medical support. The first look was of devastation to the airport buildings and then rows of burnt buildings on the road into the town. There was basic commerce such as roadside stalls selling vegetables, meat from freshly slaughtered animals, petrol in open containers and basic clothing. There were no shops because they had all been burnt. The local people appeared stressed but cheerful and welcoming because we meant relief from the past and promise for the future. The children were ear-to-ear smiles and laughter at the exotic sight of the Australian military.

Our first trip off the base was three to four hours by Land Rover up a rough unsealed road, through the dense rainforest, between shanty villages full of laughing children and into the highlands south of Dili to provide medical aid to a distressed local village. The clinic was held in a church and a Catholic seminary surrounded by dense foliage and a vibrant garden of flowers and trees with multiple coloured variegated leaves. There was a nativity scene because it was Christmas. There were a multitude of dogs and people in colourful clothes, many playing games of volleyball and basketball. Bob Marley T-shirts were particularly popular with young men. Sixty people were expected for the clinic but two hundred arrived. The clinic was well organised, everyone waited patiently and we eventually treated them all.

Our next trip was along the coast to the east of Dili for about 90 minutes to put a dressing into the eye socket of a young boy who had lost his eye during the riots. We had the same sights of lush greenery, burnt out villages and people getting their lives back into order. The population was more numerous with many pedestrians, overloaded buses with passengers hanging out of the doors and sitting on the roof and motorbikes carrying four or five people. We ate lunch on a beach that would have done justice to any tourist brochure in the world while we watched the Timorese catch fish by building long rows of stones that trapped the fish as the tide receded.

One morning we attended mass at the local Catholic Church, which gave a heart-warming insight into life returning to normal after a bad period. The local citizens wore their best Sunday clothes that were old but good quality and the statement being made by their wearers was apparent. There were no Bob Marley T-shirts in church. The service included beautiful, harmonised singing and announcements of many engagements and impending marriages confirming their optimism for the future.

East Timor was a little more secure at the time of my second deployment and so there was more freedom of movement such as walks around the airport, climbs up the neighbouring heights and group runs that provided exercise and a good look at country and people. The huge smiles and laughter of the little children showed that our curiosity of each other was mutual.

Even more interesting was a trip to the east of the country with the occupational health physician to inspect water supplies and sewerage treatment at the location of the various other deployed units from Thailand, the Philippines and South Korea. My mental images of the country persist. The roads were in disrepair but wound up and down mountain ranges that extended into the sea. Our road ran close to beautiful beaches in the valleys between the ranges but then wound up steep mountains and cliffs and back down to the next valley and beach. The plants were lush and green and became more so as we travelled east as far as Bachau and then Los Palos. There were streams and waterfalls running down the gullies. Rice was being cultivated in the flat valley regions. Chickens and dogs were running loose. Several farmers rode horses instead of the ubiquitous motorbikes. We passed through villages with huts with thatched roofs. The villagers were getting back to normal life with roadside markets, children playing and, in one village, we had to allow an elaborate wedding procession to pass by before we could continue our journey. Nonetheless, observation beyond the day-to-day life revealed that many of the public buildings, shops and churches had been burnt. There was an undamaged church in one village and we were told that the local bishop had paid money to the militia so that they left it unharmed.

The cemeteries had a mixture of white and black headstones and we were told that the black ones were the graves of victims who had been killed during Indonesian rule. There were many rumours of Indonesian harshness. We were told that they regularly checked the hospital for Timorese who were wounded during conflicts between Timorese and Indonesian soldiers. The wounded were removed and allegedly ended up in a grave with a black cross. I do not believe that any of the rumours were substantiated but, certainly, there were intermittent discoveries of unidentified victims in mass graves.

The hostile militia and insurgents were largely under control by the time of my third deployment to East Timor and so security requirements and movement around Dili had been further relaxed. The combination of unemployment, inactive militia and dependence on UN governance had resulted in an increase in local crime and disorder with local gangs making life unpleasant for local citizens. We were still able to get out and about but had to be cautious when we went to crowded areas such as the local market which was acres of closely packed stalls with every form of local product imaginable. The affluence of visiting military and aid workers contrasted with the poverty of the local citizens and we were targets for stall keepers and thieves.

The travel highlight of this deployment was west to Batugade in a huge Mack tanker truck with an equally huge tanker trailer that was transporting water to the Australian Army deployment located on the border of East and West Timor. There was discussion between the stores and the driver as to whether it was ten tonnes overweight or only eight tonnes overweight. Volunteers were needed to accompany the driver because of 'pot-shots' at the trucks. These were described as steel blow darts that the villagers were firing into the tyres of the trucks in protest that they were going through the villages too fast and not giving the kids presents. We were supposed to be accompanied by the Brazilian Military Police in a Land Cruiser for security and as guides but they did not arrive and so we departed unaccompanied. It was at this stage that I learnt that the driver had only been in the army for a short time and had little experience with the huge articulated truck. He had not been to Batugade and did not know the way. I had bought a map of Timor from Map World in Sydney for my own information. Fortunately, I had brought it with me for the truck trip otherwise we would have been lost.

The Mack truck had had a hard life in East Timor. The clutch was slipping and it had a crash gearbox that almost needed a sledgehammer to change gears. The road was narrow and it was impossible to pass or overtake. It was essential to blast the horn to scare off anything coming from the opposite direction because the road was effectively one lane even without the potholes, crumbling edges, twists, turns, ascents, descents and repaired flimsy bridges. The driver physically fought the truck all the way because of the weight.

We had big problems in Liquica. The corners were tight, the roads were confusing, there were no road signs and so we missed the turn-off to Batugade. We were trapped pointing down a steep hill in a narrow cul-de-sac. The combined Mack and trailer were impossible to reverse because the trailer had a steering front axle resulting in four sets of wheels that could go in four different directions while reversing. Add the weight, the slipping clutch and the brakes of the rear wheels staying locked after they were released and everything was a mess. At one point, it looked as though we would have to call for assistance to tow us out but the driver managed to lock the front axle of the trailer and reverse out with loud screeches of stressed tyres and metal.

We completed the difficult trip of steep hills, narrow roads, hairpin bends and suicidal oncoming traffic. We spent a lot of time in bottom gear and low ratio with the engine bellowing at full revolutions but only travelling 5kph. We arrived in Batugade after five hours. The main compensation was seeing the magnificent East Timorese scenery. The trip back in the empty truck was much easier.

I also managed a helicopter trip on this deployment. The helicopter evacuations had been contracted to a civilian service and I was invited onto one of their maintenance flights used to calibrate computers, instruments and sensors. It provided wonderful aerial views of Dili, mainland East Timor and the islands north of Dili.

Generally, exploration of the host country of the deployment was limited to short excursions outside the barracks. This was the case in Rwanda and Bougainville though in Rwanda, we were allowed a few days at the end of the deployment to see the sights of Nairobi and I took a most memorable overnight train trip to Mombasa, spent a day exploring the fascinating city and then returned by air. We also had a few days at the end of the Vanimo, PNG, deployment when we went to the local beach and later hitchhiked a flight on an army aircraft to Wewak and had a look around. The local hospital was administered by a remarkable woman who was a surgeon and a leading figure in the Catholic Church. The anaesthetist and I were privileged to operate on some of her patients who needed specialised orthopaedic treatment.

The deployment to the Solomon Islands was more relaxed and there was more freedom of movement into the city of Honiara and around the camp. The weather was hot, rainy and humid but sitting at the local beach was more enjoyable and I had a favourite log where I could sit and relax. The climate was different from the main area of the camp with a 20-knot beautifully cool breeze straight off the sea. The temperature rose about fifty metres inland from the beach and the climate immediately became hot, windless, humid and unpleasant. I was always alone and was surprised that no one else enjoyed the beach. It may have been because of the crocodiles. Swimming was banned because crocodiles were frequently seen swimming in the ocean and it was gospel that one was particularly dangerous. I chatted with the PNG soldiers about the crocodiles and they were amused that people were concerned about it. They said that in PNG the crocodiles found in the sea never attack anyone but those in the rivers are more aggressive and attack humans.

The big travel thrill of the Solomon Islands was a flight on a Caribou for rotation of police to a small island called Rennell due south of Guadalcanal. The Caribou is a remarkable aircraft that can land on an airstrip the size of a football field which was fortunate because this was the size of Tinggoa airfield where we landed. The island appeared flat from the air and about a third of it was covered by a lake that did not appear to be connected to the ocean. Presumably, the water seeped into an underground system as each village had a communal well.

The pilot 'buzzed' the short-grassed airstrip a number of times to get the children and livestock off the runway and then landed and taxied to the side with ecstatic children running alongside in great excitement. They then proudly sat on the wheels and struts from the time of our arrival until departure some hours later.

Once on land and walking around the island, it was found to be much more undulating than expected with rock hard ground thickly covered by vegetation and without the mud I anticipated from the constant rain. The buildings were professionally built wooden structures and there were substantial civic buildings such as a medical clinic, police station and a secondary school.

We returned to the Caribou to find jubilant children swarming all over the wheels, undercarriage and ramp of the aircraft beaming from ear to ear. They knew the routine and scattered once preparations for take-off were completed. The Caribou is such a simple aircraft that such a relaxed attitude could do it no harm. We took off with the rear ramp opened. We fitted harnesses, sat with our legs dangling over the edge while we flew over at low altitude and got magnificent views of the beautiful Solomon Islands looking like a travel agent's brochure of the South Pacific.

These trips were in contrast to the deployments to Iraq and Afghanistan where I was confined to the barracks and the only view of the country was through the security fencing. This was frustrating when considering the wealth of interest that exists in both countries. Iraq is the cradle of civilisation and has the artefacts to match. Afghanistan had the reputation of the friendliest and most interesting of countries for travellers before the Soviet invasion in 1979.

The view through the wire in Iraq was of flat dusty ground with sparse cultivation that was being worked by farmers using hand equipment. Viewing through binoculars revealed non-descript buildings in the far distance.

Everything was red in Afghanistan. The ground was red and red dust coated all structures. It was possible to climb security watchtowers and see villages and individual houses that were built like mini-fortresses with surrounding walls. The flat ground was a level river valley that abruptly extended into a rugged mountain range that provided a dramatic backdrop to the scene. There was some vegetation along the river but nowhere else. The location was typical of Afghanistan with a dramatic mixture of high mountains with rivers and valleys.

Because many of the deployments were into war zones, there were numerous opportunities to witness the paraphernalia of modern warfare. The deployments were the result of battlefield conflicts and the effects were in your face. This was most visible in Balad, Iraq, which was the Iraqi air force's academy and so had been targeted by the Americans early in the conflict. The base was littered with MIG aircraft that had been shot to pieces and were in various levels of destruction. They had been covered with interesting American graffiti. There were burnt out tanks and other military vehicles lying around or in huge dumps. The concrete shelters for the aircraft were covered with many small craters of different sizes depending on the weapon that fired the projectile. In contrast, there were no signs of recent battle at the Tarin Kowt base in Afghanistan, though the airfield buildings at Kandahar had an unhealthy smattering of missile craters.

Rwanda showed evidence of the conflict that had occurred about 12 months prior to my arrival. All public buildings and some private buildings had many signs of being sprayed by small arms with pockmarks and smashed windows. There were horrible unhealed machete wounds to limbs still festering after the massacres. There were old gunshot wounds that had resulted in the loss of bone and destruction of nerve and muscle sufficient to make the limb lifeless and useless.

Bougainville showed what happens when civil war causes a functioning society to stop progressing and then regress. The world had stopped for ten years in Bougainville. This was revealed most visibly by the jungle devouring man-made structures. I recall how I was asked to observe an area of jungle that looked different from any other area. It slowly became apparent that areas of the jungle were square or rectangular about the same size as a house. Indeed, they were houses where the residents had been murdered and their possessions looted. The houses had been left to rot and the jungle had swarmed all over the buildings leaving square shaped jungle as the only hint that previously there had been buildings. Scraping away the soil near the buildings revealed good quality tiles where allegedly the local mayor's body had laid after he had been assassinated.

East Timor had similar gunshot divots out of buildings and numerous burnt-out shells of buildings. It was said that the militia had used hoses from petrol tankers to douse the buildings with petrol and then set fire to them. The roads were also damaged and scarcely negotiable but it was uncertain whether this was war damage or routine lack of maintenance. The conflict had also had an effect on the local residents with fear and insecurity showing in emotions, facial expressions and body language. The destruction and sombre moods became less noticeable on successive deployments but did not disappear completely.

There were also opportunities to see remnants of past wars.

In Bougainville, there were memorials consisting of wrecked Japanese Zero fighters from World War II with twisted wings and propellers mounted on plinths and other derelict examples of military equipment.

In East Timor, we visited the memorial for 'Sparrow Force' that was a World War II Australian Army commando unit that stayed behind in East Timor when all other forces had left. They lasted for a considerable period of time with support from the local civilians and provided active resistance to the Japanese invasion. They were eventually caught and executed.

The island of Guadalcanal in the Solomon Islands was particularly interesting because it was the scene of one of the definitive battles between the US and Japan during World War II. Discussion between Australians and Americans regarding where the Japanese were first defeated on land will create an argument about the credentials of Milne Bay and Guadalcanal for this distinction. Both points of view have validity. The battle between the Japanese and Australian Armies in Milne Bay from 25 August 1942 until 7 September 1942 was the first time that the Japanese lost a land-based battle against Allied forces and so is highly significant. The battle for Guadalcanal started on 7 August 1942 and finished with the departure of the Japanese from Guadalcanal on 9 February 1943. It was the first time that allied (primarily US) forces displaced the Japanese from an island that they had occupied and so signified the turning point of the war in the Pacific. Interestingly, the division of areas of operations by the Americans meant that the battle for the Solomon Islands was under the command and control of Admiral Nimitz of the US Navy and not General MacArthur of the US Army.

One of the highlights of the deployment to the Solomon Islands was a battlefield tour run by an ex-pat Australian from Brisbane whose main job was his computer business. He took us on an extended walking tour of various major battlefields such as Red Beach (so called because of the blood in the water at the end of the battle), Sea Horse Hill, Running Horse Hill (both named because of the shape of the hills when viewed from a distance) and Bloody Ridge (no explanation needed). He also showed areas of minor skirmishes and contacts. The conditions were difficult for our walking tour with heat, humidity, frogs, lizards, leeches and steep climbs that took our breath away. I cannot comprehend how fighting men managed to run up the same steep slopes carrying full combat equipment while an entrenched enemy was firing at them.

The battle lasted for months and advantage seesawed from one side to the other. The key asset was Henderson Airfield that was originally built by the Japanese, but then taken over by the Americans soon after it was completed and held by them for the duration of the battle.

There were fascinating remnants of the battle such as a dugout used by a Japanese lookout who reported the movement of ships in the harbour. The Americans knew that he was there and spent ages looking for him but were not successful because of his ingenious hiding spot on a bluff overlooking the harbour. The Americans concentrated their search in the abundant jungle around the bluff which was the logical site for a hiding place but the shrewd lookout had created a cleverly disguised dugout in an open area that was the least likely place. Elsewhere, there were remnants of trenches and fortifications.

We walked through several villages that had been built on some of the battlefields and the residents were running a lively trade in military hardware such as spent bullets and shells, old rifles, parts from artillery and such like.

Guadalcanal was not just a land battle. Sea supply to both sides was essential and had to occur in a confined area of the Pacific Ocean. Clashes and sea battles were frequent and many ships were sunk. The Savo Sound harbour was eventually nicknamed Ironbottom Sound acknowledging the number of ships that were lying at the bottom of the sea. There were about five or six sunk wrecks that had come to rest on the foreshore and beaches around Honiara. Similarly, there were many bitter air battles between the US and Japanese fighting aircraft and their wreckage still lies in the jungle.

Memorials to the battle had been erected by both the Japanese and the USA after the war. The contrast between these memorials was fascinating.

The Japanese were the first to erect memorials and these became evident only when walking through the jungle around the battlefields. The memorial at Red Beach was a typical example. This battle occurred when the Japanese infantry charged a set defensive position of US forces across the beach. They attacked in waves and suffered heavy casualties each time. The Japanese units usually consisted of soldiers from a single village in Japan and so, if a unit suffered heavy casualties, then the village back in Japan had lost many of their sons. These villages frequently arranged memorials to the lost souls of their sons at the site of the battle or the Japanese government did so on their behalf. The memorials were spiritual in nature and were homage to departed souls rather than memorials to the war itself. There is a subtle distinction between Japanese memorials that are respectful to departed spirits and souls and western war memorials that are more commemorative to the wars and battles themselves. One is not better or more appropriate than the other. They just have a different emphasis.

We found the Japanese memorial when we were following a twisting trail through the jungle to Red Beach. We turned a corner and there it was. It was a simple stone column about five metres tall with Japanese inscriptions on it. It was plain and stark. It was hidden in the jungle and could only be seen when someone happened to walk down a remote track to a remote beach. We found a number of similar memorials in the other battlefields hidden away in the jungle.

There was no American memorial for the Battle of Guadalcanal for many years but then there was a comment on the irony that the Japanese had built memorials on the site of the battle where their fortunes had reversed and yet there were no American memorials to signify their success. That has been rectified in a major way and a most significant and respectful memorial has been built that is just as American as much as the Japanese memorials are Japanese. It is a large paved area on an elevation that provides views of most of the land battlefields, the airfield and the harbour. It provides visibility of the battles in the sea, on the land and in the air. I found this memorial just as moving as the Japanese memorials.

Chapter 17
Local Citizens

One of the pleasures of visiting faraway exotic locations is meeting the local residents and learning about their way of life. The opportunity to do this is both increased and decreased while on a military deployment. Increased because deployment is linked to the well-being and safety of the local inhabitants and so they are drawn towards the foreign visitors in uniform who represent optimism for a better future. Decreased because there would be no need for a military presence if all was secure with freedom of meeting and greeting. Security measures require a degree of separation between locals and visitors. A welcoming response from locals cannot be guaranteed because many people can resent interference from overseas countries even if their intention is to provide assistance. Overall, my experience has been warm welcomes and expressions of appreciation on my deployments.

The faces of the people of Rwanda had many expressions reflective of their multitude of emotions after their horrific experiences. There were unhappy faces with heads hanging down and looking at the ground. It could be difficult to make eye contact and, if eye contact was achieved and greeted with a smile, the smiles were wan and half-hearted done out of politeness rather than happiness. It was as though there was a massive communal suffering of extreme post-traumatic stress disorder. Tutsi and Hutu were easy to distinguish because of their contrasting physical features but both ethnic groups appeared equally traumatised. The Hutus had massacred the Tutsi and then the Tutsi Rwandan Patriotic Army had invaded and commenced revenge massacring of Hutus. There was universal mourning for lost loved ones and universal fear for the future.

There were also happier and more optimistic faces such as the young man who gave me a lift on the back of his bicycle during our 'City to Surf' run in Kigali. People were getting back to normal life and commerce with hope for a better life over the horizon. The women were returning to the many beauty salons in the city. Children with beaming smiles were squealing with delight as they played with their makeshift toys such as old bicycle wheels that they rolled with sticks and then chased them as they sped down the street. They could not hide their curiosity and delight at the sight of overseas soldiers and their trusting approach to us was moving. Many were orphans being looked after by neighbours, relatives or older siblings.

We visited Mother Teresa's orphanage in Kigali and saw the best and worst of humanity. The orphanage was run by delightful young nurses from India who were all bright smiles and blue and white nun's habits. The residents were little children who had lost their parents in the massacre but they were all clean, well fed, well clothed, very polite, happy and with a huge variety of faces and expressions. We watched a school lesson and saw the excitement and laughter of little children living in the present with no knowledge of the past and no thoughts of the future. An adjoining section of the orphanage housed disabled adolescents and young adults such as a 21-year-old man with no hands because they had been blown off by a mine. He had lost all independence. He struggled to eat using a spoon clutched between the stumps of his forearms. He was embarrassed by his useless stumps and spent most of his time with his arms in his pockets so that people could not see them. He was one of many with similar problems.

The Kigali market revealed another facet of Rwandan life. It was located in a huge wooden and corrugated iron construction sheltering stalls that were wall-to-wall and spilling out onto the neighbouring streets. It was mayhem. The stalls were colourful, merchandise piled on more merchandise, noisy, smelly and hopelessly crowded with vendors touting their wares in top voice and the throng of customers bartering equally loudly. All imaginable items were for sale. Cosmetics, clothes, wigs, food, vegetables, tinned food, fruit, animals being slaughtered and hacked up on the spot, rotting fish, cooking utensils, shoes, cigarettes, postcards, pots, American dollars and much more. Tempers could be short. One man was carrying a bundle of about ten trussed up live chickens and this prompted a loud complaint from a bystander that escalated into a major slanging match amongst all and sundry. I have no idea what it was all about but I am sure that it was not about 'animal rights'.

The deployment to Vanimo, Papua New Guinea, brought us closer to the local citizens like no other because of the nature of the disaster and the purpose of the mission. This has been detailed elsewhere in this book in the descriptions of the deployment and no further amplification is necessary. Suffice to say the locals were friendly, helpful, accommodating, cheerful and grateful. My main memory is of big smiles and colourful clothing. We were based some distance from the tsunami zone and so this memory is not representative of the distress and misfortune of those directly involved in the disaster. Tragedy and absence of law enforcement bring out the worst in some people in all countries and sadly this occurred in the disaster area with violent assaults, some of which were sexual, and thieving of personal property.

My main contact with local citizens in Bougainville was through our provision of medical aid. Bougainvilleans are said to have the darkest skin of any race and I did not see anything to disprove this. Again, the superficial impression was of colourful clothing, big welcoming smiles and gratitude for the assistance provided. The impression was of a national sigh of relief after ten grim years of war between complex groups with constantly changing allegiances. These groups perceived the PNG Government as their common enemy but this did not stop them from fighting amongst themselves.

Infrastructure and personal housing had been destroyed but were being renewed. Public services were resuming with limited resources. There was an underlying impression of sadness and continuing grieving which is to be expected following a conflict that resulted in 15,000 to 20,000 deaths in an island with a population of about 175,000. People's lives had been on hold for ten years and were just resuming.

There were some memorable characters. I very briefly met revolutionary leaders Samuel Kauona and Francis Ona at different times and their strength of personality was unmistakable.

A less high-profile character was the man who owned the Bougainville airstrip. I had the privilege of witnessing 'Bob Marley' tending to the agricultural parts of his land next to the runway while we waited to depart at the end of the deployment. I was told that all land on Bougainville had a designated private owner and the owner of the runway had hit the jackpot because he was being paid considerable rent. I first saw him dressed in a tropical shirt, baggy shorts, sandals and flowing locks of hair. He was nicknamed 'Bob Marley' because of his devotion to the reggae singer and had copied his hair and appearance. He was never seen without a Bob Marley T-shirt. He was not unique. Bob Marley was hugely popular in all of the Pacific countries where I deployed. He owned the land where the airstrip was located and was prodding the ground around the airstrip with hand tools to cultivate his crops. It was rumoured that he was being paid handsomely for the use of his land for the airstrip and he had rocketed up the Bougainvillean social order.

The most interesting aspect of the interaction with the East Timorese was the steady change from a war-torn country to a reconstructing country by the time of my second deployment and then to a functioning society on my third deployment. The first deployment was all burnt out buildings and cars while the third deployment was more normal commerce and social interaction.

The opportunities for direct contact with local East Timorese were very limited on the first deployment because of security concerns. Most impressions came from observation from a distance. We mixed on three occasions that have already been described; firstly, the humanitarian clinic managed by the Singaporeans, secondly, a journey along the coast to dress the eye socket of a young boy who had suffered an eye injury and thirdly, attendance at a church service. All gave the impression of a traumatised populace that was getting comfort by trying to resume a normal life.

There were more opportunities to mix with local residents on the second deployment. We ran through local villages and residential areas with the Hash House Harriers and could see men working in cottage industries, in agriculture in the fields, women cooking, washing and clothes making and children laughing and playing with makeshift toys such as the universally popular bike wheels and sticks. We saw the first graduates from the new police school. There we were treated to speeches by UN dignitaries and demonstrations of marching, martial arts and motorbike driving by the new graduates.

We bought carvings and ornaments from markets catering to overseas visitors looking for memorabilia. We visited the local market that was very similar to the one in Kigali except that it did not have the large shelter. The traditional highly coloured cloth of East Timor was particularly appealing. At the time of my third deployment to East Timor, there was talk of closing and dismantling the market because it had become a hotbed of crime and a meeting point for various gangs and undesirables.

The nature of the deployment to Balad, Iraq, meant there was almost no personal interaction with local Iraqis. Security was tight. Saddam Hussein's army, police and secret intelligence agencies had been disbanded and were mixed with the local populace. Overtly unfriendly Iraqis were easy to distinguish because they were the ones that joined the insurgents and fired mortars and rockets at us.

Friendly Iraqis were much more difficult to confirm because friend and foe were mixed together.

Times were financially tough for the Iraqis and so they were keen to get employment on the base. The screening was difficult and it was known that some of the local employees were informants for the insurgents. One was found with maps of the base structures hidden in his clothing. It was discovered that another was a former commander of the base and he was using his access to note the changes that had been made and the locations of vital equipment. The situation was not helped when a suicide bomber, dressed in Iraqi security forces uniform, exploded in a US Army base with many fatalities.

Relationships with Iraqis were, therefore, cautious and suspicious and I did not get to know them personally. The overall impression was of quiet respect and a rather passive approach to life. Undoubtedly, the sudden and rapid upheavals in Iraqi life had affected their demeanour. For many, their whole world had collapsed around them and there seemed to be a little uncertainty whether our arrival was an advantage over their previous situation. Saddam Hussein's Ba'ath system of government had similarities to the Soviet centralised system with all power and decisions being referred upwards step by step until the highest level was reached. This had resulted in fear of making decisions in the lower management levels and the indecision and lack of initiative seemed to have become ingrained in their culture. The overall impression was of intelligence, respectfulness and a unique sophisticated culture but rendered passive and ineffective by fear and insecurity. It is difficult for a surgeon to motivate the injured to recover if all they want to do is lie around in bed and wait for someone else to do the recovering for them.

Iraqi elections were held while I was in Balad and this produced some improvement in confidence but random bombings throughout the country kept morale very low. There was changing character in the police force with recruiting of new personnel. The previous police force was disbanded because the members were basically gangsters and were heavily involved in extortion, kidnapping, murder, theft, corruption and generally enforcing Saddam's mad regime. They would run when the police stations were attacked by insurgents but the new recruits were standing and fighting with some success, killing and capturing the opposition. Future events indicate that this improvement was not sustained.

I never had a chance to see Iraq outside of the USAF base in Balad but managed to get some insight from the experiences of others.

One example was a wounded US soldier who was being treated for wounds received when he was in the Sunni triangle of Iraq near the Syrian border. He was in a Bradley troop carrier at the tail end of a patrol driving through a town when someone stepped out of a crowd and threw a parachute grenade at his vehicle. He was pessimistic as to whether the US would ever succeed in his sector. He said that the people hated the US for all sorts of different reasons and they now felt disenfranchised because of the election. None of the locals voted. He said that only 400 voted in one sector and they were the Iraqi National Guard who were preserving security. The US Army had to secure one voting venue with an armed helicopter because it was being attacked by insurgents. He said that US troops were attacked regularly and all of the locals knew what was happening and knew the insurgents. The US soldiers knew they were about to be attacked whenever the streets suddenly became completely deserted. The average local Iraqi was struggling to survive from one day to the next because of lack of work and money. They were unable to look to the future because all of their energy was committed to day-to-day survival. The local sheikhs were very wealthy and were paying about one month's wages to someone to fire an RPG at the Americans. This was good value to someone who was impoverished and unemployed. It then became a blood feud if they were shot by the US soldiers who were defending themselves and so the cycle continued. None of the locals was prepared to open any form of commerce such as a store because of the insecurity. Consequently, no one had any form of commitment to the country and they would fight whoever was in power. His description was that this troubled area was only a small part of the country but "it was cancer which will eventually kill the country". He said that the Iraqis regarded the US Army as weak because they were not destructive. As an example of different standards, he said that once a small town in Syria did something that was unacceptable to President Bashar Al Assad of Syria and his reaction was to take as much artillery as was available and to shell the town until it was completely flattened. He said the civilians in his area could not understand why the US did not do the same to them and they interpreted this as a sign of weakness.

I later had an interesting discussion with an Iraqi national who worked as an interpreter on base and resided in Balad. He was more optimistic and said that things were getting much better outside. He said a factor was George W Bush winning re-election. Previously people were concerned that the US would leave Iraq and there would be reprisals against those who assisted them as happened in 1991 when the US did not push on to Baghdad and Saddam stayed in control.

He said that the election on 30 January 2005 had also given people much more confidence to assist the security forces. Previously, they were afraid to inform on the insurgents even though "everyone knew who they were and where they lived" but now it was possible to inform in anonymity and know that there would be no reprisals. He said that the people who carry out the acts were Iraqis but they were led by outsiders such as Syrians. They were paid money each time they did something, such as US$100 to fire a mortar bomb into Balad base which was good money for someone who had very little. He said the town of Balad was much more secure because US troops had sealed the perimeter and Iraqi forces were going through the town and clearing out and arresting insurgents. The locals increased confidence in informing had made a big difference. Overall, he felt that things were improving substantially but there was still quite a way to go. Sadly, events over the years following have disproved his optimism.

I had an informative conversation with a data analysis expert attached to a US Army psychology team touring the country to try to assess attitudes of the Iraqis. He did not believe that Iraq would reach true democratic self-governing for some time, partly because one of the features of their past society was that it was much centralised. All power existed in the central government in Baghdad and the role of local councils or their equivalent was to implement the policy. They had no power or flexibility and it was difficult to get these officials to take decisions or show independence. They always desired to go back to the central seat of power which was now the Americans. The country had become very passive and dependent on the Americans and this attitude would continue with the recently elected Iraqi government. He said that the local people had been very positive and excited about the election because they had had nothing like it before. In previous elections, they received voting slips at the same time that they received their ration vouchers. The choice consisted of whether you wanted Saddam or not and had to be filled out in front of the official at the booth. Unsurprisingly, Saddam had received a 99.7% approval vote. I can only guess what happened to the 0.3% who voted against him. Iraq was a socialised 'welfare state' under Saddam. The Ba'ath Party had a policy of elevating the importance of State and downplaying the importance of religion and intellectualism, reflecting their links with the Soviets at the formation of the Ba'ath Party. The end result was that the people were very dependent on government handouts and regarded anything they received as a right and not a benefit. The outcome was inert and apathetic citizens who tended to sit back and wait for someone to do the job for them. This description matched many of the patients we were treating.

There was similar high security and lack of access to Afghan civilians during the deployment to Tarin Kowt, Afghanistan. There was some contact through interpreters, civilian casualties treated in the hospital and vendors at the occasional markets on base. The overall impression was of a more aggressive and violent persona than the average Iraqi. With very little evidence, I formed the idiosyncratic opinion that the passive nature of suicide bomber suited the national characteristic of the Iraqi insurgent while the Afghan insurgent took the more aggressive role of an attacker with AK47 and knife. There was also an impression that Afghan society was more primitive and impoverished in comparison to the more complex and sophisticated Iraqi society. Family ties and tribal loyalty were very strong in Afghanistan. This was a country that was extraordinarily welcoming to foreigners prior to the Soviet invasion in 1979. It was the darling of the 60s and 70s hippie set.

We did not view events with the same perspective as the Afghans. An example occurred when a young Afghan presented to the Emergency Department scarcely alive and soon succumbing to fatal knife wounds inflicted by his cousin. We asked the Afghan interpreter why the man had murdered his cousin and, to our disbelief, he stated that the man had insulted the cousin's father. Our inability to understand a society that accepts such an extreme punishment out of proportion to the crime was matched by the interpreter's disbelief that we could not see the rationality behind the deed. He regarded the cousin's action as essential to preserve the honour of his father.

One of the ironies of the Middle Eastern deployments is that I learnt more about Americans than Iraqis in Balad and more about the Dutch than Afghans in Tarin Kowt.

Chapter 18
Australian and Allied Defence Forces

The Oxford Dictionary definition of camaraderie is 'mutual trust and friendship among people who spend a lot of time together'. My addition to the definition is 'a desire to see your comrades succeed and willingness to help them succeed'. The word defines the best aspects of personal relationships between ADF members while on deployment. The bond is even stronger because each team member has a role to play and failure of one human component of the unit can mean that the whole structure fails. Good team members on an ADF deployment realise that success or failure can depend on their own efforts and on the support that they provide to the other members. Conversely, if one of the team members is struggling or fragile, it can be disastrous if the other members do not provide support or, worse still, take steps to destabilise the struggling member.

The level of this camaraderie and support was one of the most enriching aspects of being on deployment and is something that does not occur in civilian life and perhaps can only be understood by someone who has been on a military deployment.

The Latin word 'frater' translates as 'brother' and so the word 'fraternisation' must suggest 'brotherhood' or at least some sort of relationship that implies brotherly love. In the ADF, it has somehow come to mean a romantic or sexual relationship between ADF members while on deployment and is strictly banned for all sorts of good reasons. I never witnessed it occurring though this may be more a comment on my lack of observation rather than the reality of human nature. I did hear of a genuine romance between two officers that continued after the deployment and resulted in marriage and joint careers when they left the ADF but my knowledge does not extend beyond that. In fact, members 'live in each other's pockets' while on deployment because of the close living and working arrangements, thus confounding the logistics of creating an illicit relationship.

Generally, everybody worked and relaxed comfortably together and this can be attributed to a number of factors such as the personal strengths of those deployed, the self-discipline that comes with military training and the quality of the commanding officers on the deployment. Nonetheless, the times were stressful and inevitably some nerves became a bit frayed around the edges. This could cause some troublesome times between members. A person could become snappy when talking to colleagues, uncooperative when tractability is required or rude and grumpy. Some simply withdrew to their room when not working and this would cause anxiety amongst concerned colleagues. This could be more noticeable in deployments that were less busy, leaving more time for introspection. It is a tough call for colleagues to be understanding when they are stretched to their limit and with little time to provide supportive therapy.

Separation from loved ones can be a factor, particularly during long deployments and unexpected extensions. There can be stress on the longest and most secure relationship and some did not survive the separation. Sometimes, the relationship was nearing its end and the deployment was the catalyst for the final decision. Shorter relationships do not get much attention but these are important for the individuals involved. I recall speaking to one young woman in her early 20s who had met a young man a few weeks before her deployment. The relationship was just starting to blossom when they were separated by her deployment and she had not heard from him since. She related wistfully how she had speculated on a shared life with the young man and she felt that the opportunity had vanished without her getting a fair chance.

In some ways, a deployment was a microcosm as to how we cope with life. Some modify their behaviour to match circumstances and some try to modify circumstances to match their personality. The former is more suited to a deployment and the latter is likely to get the label of 'high maintenance'.

The interaction with defence forces from friendly allies was one of the most interesting aspects of deployments.

Rwanda was the location of the most impressive and unforgettable forces of all, namely the Ghurkhas. They were few in number but highly visible. They had been tasked to provide security for the UN personnel and UN headquarters. I am not sure whether they were hired directly by the UN or whether they were part of the UK defence force. They were short in stature but appeared to pack more muscle than someone twice their height. Their body builds matched Clive James' description of a condom filled with walnuts. My first contact was when a group of us entered the main gate of the UN headquarters where the Ghurkhas were on sentry duty. We each presented our ADF ID card and were each in turn subjected to this extraordinary long penetrating glare from hard black eyes set in a face that appeared to be polished brown granite. I felt as if the eyes were boring into my head, reading my thoughts and deciding that I was a deceitful imposter. It was unnerving. There was a complete change in demeanour once we had all passed this intense scrutiny. The granite face beamed, the bundle of muscles sprang into attention and produced the most magnificently professional salute I have ever seen. The transformation from hostility to welcome was dramatic. I often wonder what the reaction would have been if we had not passed the initial scrutiny.

My next vision of Ghurkhas was watching them play volleyball dressed in shorts and singlet. It confirmed they were 90% muscle and extraordinarily fit and athletic. It appeared that they had springs or little rockets attached to their shoes because they jumped about three times their body height with no apparent effort. It seemed physically impossible. They also shone in the Kigali City to Surf run which was won by a Ghurkha who looked even more indestructible than the others.

There were units from many countries scattered throughout Rwanda but we had little contact with them. The mixture of nations was demonstrated at a large parade to present UN medals to the various contingents. Military forces from Zambia, Senegal, India, Gambia, Uganda and Australia marched in and lined up in excellent order. There were many dignitaries including the commanding officers of all these contingents and the overall UN commanding officer who was Canadian.

This was only a small representation of the countries that contributed troops to UNAMIR throughout its existence. Personnel were sent from Argentina, Australia, Austria, Bangladesh, Belgium, Brazil, Canada, Chad, Congo, Djibouti, Egypt, Ethiopia, Fiji, Germany, Ghana, Guinea, Guinea Bissau, Guyana, India, Jordan, Kenya, Malawi, Mali, Netherlands, Niger, Nigeria, Pakistan, Poland, Romania, Russia, Senegal, Slovakia, Spain, Switzerland, Togo, Tunisia, United Kingdom, Uruguay, Zambia and Zimbabwe.

New Zealand personnel were in Vanimo, PNG, and in Bougainville and the relationship was the traditional Kiwi and Aussie interface of sibling rivalry and camaraderie with the latter predominant. There are a few whimsical memories such as the NZ officer in Vanimo who gave us a briefing each morning as to the best direction to run to the high ground if another tsunami arrived. (The RAAF pilots advised all RAAF personnel to head for them because they claimed that they could get the Herc airborne in two minutes.) The NZ haka for the Sing-Sing and the reaction of the local women is the most vivid memory. NZ provided the helicopter pilots in Bougainville but we did not see them often. I have already described the NZ pilot who compared the advantages and disadvantages of single and twin-engine Iroquois helicopters.

I met and worked with many more foreign defence forces during the three tours to East Timor. The New Zealanders were there from the start and I visited their most impressive deployable hospital in Suai. It was small in scale but was an excellent design and suited their needs perfectly. It was designed, purchased and put together by one person and this was apparent because of the simplicity and the compatibility of all of the components. The damaging compromises of a committee had not destroyed the purity of the design.

The Singaporeans were also prominent on the first deployment to East Timor with a substantial medical unit in the hospital. They were high quality in both the military and the medical sense. They were also relaxed, particularly when off duty, and were good for the morale of the medical unit assisted by liberal prescriptions of illicit 'Singapore Slings'. Their hospitality got a little out of hand on 1999–2000 New Year's Eve much to the distress of our CO who accused the males of "pretend fraternisation" with the females. The Singaporean commanding officer was young for his high rank and the word was that he was being fast-tracked through their defence force.

The second deployment provided more opportunities to visit allied defence forces. There was a smaller Singaporean force in the hospital but they had been replaced by a much larger Egyptian army medical and surgical team that was sharing facilities and working cheek by jowl with the Australian team. There were differences in attitudes and culture which required extreme diplomacy by the RAAF officer who was the Australian CO. He managed brilliantly but with significant personal stress. The situation was not helped by the Egyptian CO living in luxury accommodation in the main city and rarely visiting the hospital. The social interaction was more cordial than the professional interaction and we were frequently invited to informative sessions and were impressed by the remarkable history of Egypt over millennia and the size and power of the Egyptian defence force. An Egyptian group sang beautifully at the farewell ceremony for the Singaporeans. We received traditional Egyptian gifts and a specialist colleague bought an Egyptian army uniform.

We gained a different perspective of the Egyptians at their medal presentation ceremony that was most interesting and great fun. Many local and deployed dignitaries of impressive status and rank arrived at the hospital amidst great pomp and ceremony. First, there was the Egyptian national anthem, then long and important speeches and then the presentation of UN medals. The Egyptians turned on entertainment of fancy marching and drill called 'silent parade'. There were rows and columns of troops overlapping and interdigitating with each other while they slapped, twirled and threw their rifles at each other. Two rifles fell over and one bayonet was thrown forwards off a rifle. Otherwise, all went well and was followed by an Egyptian dinner, a video presentation of Egyptian history and then many long films of music and dancers, belly and traditional.

This deployment was damaged when one of the New Zealand troopers was shot and killed by Timorese militia. This senseless event caused grieving and drew all contingents closer together. It was a sombre warning of the risks of deployment and reminded us that there were people out there who wanted to kill us.

We visited other contingents when a group of us travelled east in a Land Cruiser to carry out public health checks on their accommodation. Firstly, we visited Thailand's health facility in Baucau where we found innovation, professionalism and military discipline. The hospital and barrack buildings were pre-fabricated and deployable but had the appearance of permanent structures. The building frame was made from iron girders made in Thailand and shipped to East Timor. It was erected over a concrete slab and cladding attached. A well-designed combination of eaves, shutters and through ventilation maintained the temperature without air conditioning. The accommodation barracks revealed beds lined up in even spaces and made with perfectly smooth blankets, crisp sheets, kitbags under the beds, spare blankets folded on the end of the beds and pillows puffed up in a standard fashion. Every bed and its trappings looked identical and there was a complete absence of clutter. It had the appearance of the perfect military barracks.

Our next stop was in Los Palos where the South Koreans were deployed. We again found a high quality Asian military contingent with even more discipline than the Thais, most likely because South Korea remains at war with the North and the threat is increasing. Everything was done on the double, very formal and accompanied by snaps to attention and salutes. The official photographer of our group braced himself rigidly as he took the photo, called out acknowledgement and then saluted at the completion. In contrast, we were treated to a traditional Korean military dinner in the evening which was most relaxed, friendly and entertaining. It was completed with the exchange of gifts and embarrassingly the Australians got the better of the exchange. I suspect that I value my Korean military mementoes and display box of tiny carved dolls more than the Koreans value their Australian Army sew-on rising sun.

There was a greater variety of nations on the third deployment but the contacts were much more superficial, such as when we saw them as patients. We had Portuguese guards for the hospital and had a bit more contact with them such as dismantling and comparing weapons. One of our female officers developed an even closer relationship that blossomed into romance and marriage. We also saw Ghanaians, Jordanians and Bangladeshi.

We had little to do with other countries' defence forces in the Solomon Islands except for a few New Zealanders but there was a large contingent of Australian

Federal Police. They were so different from the members from the Australian Defence Force that it was almost like dealing with a force from a different country. There were contrasting standards of discipline and self-control. I have no doubt that the ADF's stricter standards kept their personnel much better prepared for the inevitable crises that occur in a peacekeeping mission.

The deployment to Balad, Iraq, was to a USAF Base and so interaction with the 25,000 US personnel on base was inevitable but was informative about how their defence force functioned. I was impressed. The size of the entire US defence force is so enormous that it cannot be conservative or unchanging or inflexible, otherwise it would fall in a heap of disorganisation. I was impressed by their ability to identify a problem, research a solution and implement it. An example of this was demonstrated during my deployment. Australia had had a number of deployments to warlike or austere environments prior to the problems in the Middle East and it had become apparent to the ADF that surgeons trained and experienced in the civilian setting were not easily adaptable to military surgery. Changes were made but it was a slow process with resistance from several quarters. It was not a quick and easy process. The US had the same issue but even more so when their conflicts in Afghanistan and Iraq commenced. They had a large number of surgeons in 'active duty' or full-time service who had been trained only in civilian style surgery when treating defence force members and their dependents. Training in military surgery had been neglected and the deficiency became apparent when the conflict started. Civilian techniques are inappropriate for the terrible blast and high-velocity gunshot wounds of battle casualties and old principles had to be re-learnt. By the time of my arrival in Balad, the problem had been acknowledged and they were already moving into remedial steps. High-level researchers were setting up information gathering systems and analysing the treatment and results. They were matching the treatment in the field, acceptable standards of military surgery and the final result. The information was already coming in by the time that I left Iraq about four months later and they were implementing changes in the training of specialists and changes in resuscitation and surgery on the battlefield. Many of these changes have now found their way into civilian practice. The US defence force health services turned their huge ship around in a few months whereas the ADF took years to turn our little canoe around.

The US serving members in the Middle East expressed pride in their defence force and US citizens reciprocate with respect and honour for their sailors, soldiers and airmen. I took many opportunities to speak with Americans in the mess, in the gym, at work and during the social and education sessions provided.

The middle management level, such as Major, Lieutenant-Colonel and senior NCO, was the most impressive of the US personnel. They had comprehensive knowledge of their particular areas of expertise and had the dynamism and initiative to put it into practice. Those members required to be the interface between the US forces and important Iraqis showed remarkable knowledge and understanding of Arabic and Muslim culture. This knowledge was mainly used for narrow 'tactical' purposes such as arranging public assistance in building, education, health, law enforcement and court cases. They also expressed opinions regarding the "strategic" aspects of western culture coping with the complexities of the Middle East, but there were no signs that their highly pertinent advice was reaching the highest political levels of the USA.

The courage of US servicemen and women impressed me during my deployment to Iraq. They had made their commitment and they accepted their lot even though they were aware of the risks. I heard no complaints that the US was going over the parapet into danger more so than their allies and their casualty rate reflected this. The helicopter pilots were particularly fearless and skilful. The stories of the casualties from ambushed patrols brought into the hospital confirmed a culture of 'pushing on' when facing direct threats. There was evidence of a moral sense of duty such as casualties being treated on merit whether friend or foe. Many were practising Christians with overt shows of praying and Bible studies, perhaps because so many were from the southern states of the USA.

An interesting assessment from one of our senior officers who had been in the theatre for quite a while was that the US trooper overall was a high-quality individual but a little conservative and unimaginative, perhaps lacking personal depth. He stated that this was a comment on the fighting quality of the US trooper and was not a statement that the campaign was going well. He said that they were having great demands put on them. The war was unusual for them in that they were in the middle of the conflict and were aware of how it was all going but then would sit at dinner and watch CNN or other TV news and hear their leaders make statements which were way off reality. Many of them were becoming cynical. The troops were aware of IEDs and other incidents that had occurred throughout the country and this sort of information had not been available to the ground troops in other wars. The troops could have their personal battle action and then hear of their comrade's problems via CNN the same night. They were tough and courageous soldiers; a lot was required of them in action and they were doing remarkably well as an army.

The training of health personnel had subtle differences from Australian training and this included the medical specialists. Our training is more on the lines of basic principles that allow a degree of flexibility to adapt to the uniqueness of the patient and the situation. This means that we have a number of options as required. The US training seemed to emphasise one 'right' solution for a given injury and often the solution was documented in a protocol. There was a reluctance to step outside these guidelines and this caused problems if the 'right' solution did not match circumstances. It worked well if the 'right' solution was indeed 'right' but ran into problems when it was wrong.

The USA is a huge country with tens of millions of people of every possible variety. Generalisations about Americans are certain to be wrong and I avoid them. Nonetheless, I believe there is a national characteristic that has developed after years of leading the world in wealth, business, inventiveness and culture amongst many other things. Americans have grown up believing that they are always right and the rest of the world is keen to learn from them. They acknowledge that the rest of the world makes insulting comments about Americans but this is only envy and deep down they all want to find out how Americans do it. Consequently, there is a culture of Americans telling everyone else what to do but with little curiosity about other countries and definitely no acknowledgement that they may do things better and Americans could learn from them.

There were stories of long deployments followed by re-deployment such as the 23-year-old who was deployed for nine months and thought that he had returned to his family for a long time. Six months later, he was re-deployed for 12 to 18 months. The long deployments were taking their toll on the Americans. One of the chaplains said that there were many marital problems associated with the long deployments of 12 months or longer. The deployment could cause the problem or unmask the problem. Financial strife was not unusual, especially if the partner at home was an uncontrolled spender, particularly with credit cards. I am convinced that deployments of one year or longer are not a good idea and are damaging to personnel.

Another interesting conversation was with a National Guardsman in his late forties or early fifties who was a Flight Engineer in Sherpa Aircraft. He was not particularly happy with his present situation because he had been planning to live six months in New Zealand and six months in the northwest USA, preferably in Washington State. He had been in the US defence forces for about 21 years before transferring to the National Guard only to be called back into full-time service with the US Army. He had been in Iraq for 10 months and had about two months left but was apprehensive that they were going to keep him in Full Time Service (FTS) when he got back to the USA because of his training. He was critical of the Sherpa, which was made in Ireland. He described it as a civilian aircraft that had no modifications for war service. The US National Guard only had about 40 of them and they were all in Iraq and he claimed they were only using them to justify replacing them. They had flown them from the USA to Iraq by a long northern route with many stopovers. Their top speed was about 180 knots and the journey took three weeks through eastern USA, Nova Scotia, Iceland, Scotland, England and across Europe. The aircraft were not pressurised and at one stage, they had to get up to 18,000 ft to cross the Alps. He said they used oxygen and it was freezing cold. The flight became even scarier once they reached the Middle East because they had no protection or warning against Surface to Air Missiles (SAM). The aircrafts automatically dropped radar-confusing flares if they were locked onto by radar sites for missiles, but this could also happen with other triggers such as base radar and even helicopter rear rotors had a frequency which could activate them. They flew at 70 feet to avoid missiles and carried two observers to spot insurgents shooting at them. He says that they were frequently shot at with small arms and RPGs and one missed him by about 50 feet. The aircraft had no armour and any hit would probably have brought them down. They often saw insurgents lining them up with missiles but they flew past too soon for them to have a shot. They were the only US aircraft that flew at low altitude for safety reasons and he was interested when I told him that the RAAF did the same in the Hercules. He felt that the risks were excessive and that the tasks he was given, such as carrying one pallet of light bulbs or two passengers who had no reason to travel, were not important enough to justify the risks.

In contrast, another National Guard pilot described the Sherpa as a "wonderful aircraft" and he was enjoying his work enormously.

The Americans were friendly to the deployed Australians and expressed considerable gratitude for the contribution by our country. It was necessary for our commanding officer and me to visit the US Army logistic office when we were looking for my missing trunk. We were first greeted by a stunningly beautiful African-American private who was all perfect figure, extreme hairdo, makeup on a beautiful face and southern drawl. She was reluctant to let us anywhere near her stores but condescended to ask her Sergeant. My heart sank when the Sergeant appeared and was a large, muscular African-American woman with arms in gunslinger posture, a ferocious frown and a glare that could pierce armour plating. We explained the problem and her expression changed to a beaming smile of flashing white teeth and she said, "Ah! You are Australians. Sure! Of course, you can go in and have a look around. We will do anything for the Aussies."

We were part of the Role 2 hospital in Tarin Kowt, Afghanistan, which was a Netherlands defence force deployment. We were an embedded unit providing operating suite and intensive care services under the command of a RAAF officer but the hospital was under the command of a Dutch officer which was similar to the arrangement in Balad. This meant that our services were controlled by the Netherlands defence force but we did not lose our autonomy. The relationship between Dutch and Australians was amicable and cooperative with the national characteristics so similar that we easily dovetailed into their system. My wife and I have remained close friends with the Dutch CO. The Dutch were relaxed, professional and competent. They set high standards when working and insisted on rest and recuperation when not on duty. The buildings, equipment and resupply resources were high quality. Some of their methods were different from the Americans partly because the facility and base were a smaller footprint than Balad. The main differences were in systems and logistics such as the availability of blood for transfusion, specialist cover, laboratory services, X-ray and allied health services. The close and harmonious relationship between Dutch and Australians made this an enjoyable deployment.

Chapter 19
Hostile Forces

For obvious reasons, we had less contact with forces that were fighting against us than with friendly forces.

The Rwandan deployment was classified as 'Non-Warlike' for many years until it was correctly assessed as more dangerous than some of the 'Warlike' deployments. It was re-classified as 'Warlike' with improvement in the entitlements of the personnel who were deployed.

Theoretically, the Rwandan Patriotic Army was not hostile to us but they were not all that friendly either. They were initially called the Rwandan Patriotic Front and were a Tutsi organisation that tried to take control of the country by force during the Rwandan Civil War in the 1980s. They had been driven back to Uganda before the Hutus massacred the Tutsi in 1994 and they resumed hostilities at that time to protect their fellow Tutsi. They had taken control of the country by July 1994, renaming themselves the Rwandan Patriotic Army, and had commenced revenge killings of Hutu by the time the UN Peacekeepers had arrived. Their frustration at never having total revenge fomented resentment towards the UN Peacekeepers, including the Australian medical team and the Australian Army infantry company who were providing security for the team. There were major and minor incidents of confrontation that could have easily provoked a response resulting in bloodshed and compromising the UN deployment.

The most significant 'incident' was the Kibeho Massacre which has been well documented in Kevin O'Halloran's book entitled *Pure Massacre*. This occurred a few weeks before my arrival in Rwanda and had caused great distress within the Australian team. The RPA herded thousands of Hutus into a refugee camp and then slowly shrank its size so that they could seize suspected murderers they believed were guilty of the massacre. The refugees became more and more concentrated in a tiny area of filth and degradation and, inevitably, they rioted as intended by the RPA. They now had their excuse and started murdering refugees with rifles, hand grenades and machetes. Four thousand refugees were killed and many more wounded as was planned by the RPA. Australian Army medical workers and infantry were present but were unable to provide protection with deadly force because of UN rules. The RPA deliberately distressed the Australians by performing acts of barbarity in their faces hoping to provoke them into returning fire with their weapons. The RPA heavily out-numbered and out-gunned the Australians and the end result would most likely have been death for most of the Australians, if not all, leaving the RPA the last man standing and able to provide a dishonest version of events with no witnesses to dispute their version. Fortunately, the Australians remained disciplined and were able to assist the casualties with their limited resources.

Another knife-edge confrontation occurred following a collision between an Australian Army Armoured Personnel Carrier (APC) and an RPA four-wheel drive vehicle as they were departing their respective barracks. The entrances were directly opposite each other across the street and a collision was always going to happen, especially considering the restricted manoeuvrability of the APC and the cavalier driving styles of the RPA. The collision was minor but the reaction of the RPA was way over the top, ranging between confiscation of the APC and arrest of the Australian occupants. At one stage, they threatened to remove the APC by force and this provoked the proportional response of Australian infantry running out of their barracks in numbers and threatening the RPA by directly aiming their rifles at them in 'action' position which is live rounds in the firing chamber and the safety catch off. Fortunately, the noise of rounds going into the chambers was enough to emphasise the seriousness of the situation and RPA officers got their men back under control, but any further escalation could have resulted in casualties.

Two of the RPA barracks were our next-door neighbours, one at the hospital and one at HQ barracks. It was a bit like living uncomfortably with a grumpy neighbour who seems to cause trouble no matter how hard you try to be neighbourly. There was always a suspicion that they were trying to provoke armed conflict with UN troops and some of the methods of provocation were ugly. They knew that our sentries used night vision goggles and some of the ugliest incidents, such as torture or summary execution, were deliberately on the street and in their view during the night. Imagine the distress at being deployed to protect the citizens of a county and then see them killed without being able to do anything about it because of UN 'Rules of Engagement'.

My first knowledge of the RPA was just before dawn on my first morning in Kigali. I awoke to the sound of beautifully musical chanting by men that evoked romantic images of Africa. The harmony and rhythm of the sound were both rousing and moving. It was a company of RPA fighters doing fitness training by running around the suburban streets of Kigali particularly in the vicinity of UN barracks. These were tall athletes running effortlessly in synchronisation with their chanting. It was impressive, visually and audibly, and I looked forward to the spectacle every morning. Later, I found out that the translation of the chants was a fairly graphic description of what they would like to do to UN personnel. Once they amused themselves by throwing a stone through our window and we were instructed to grovel on the floor until it could be confirmed that it was not a hand grenade.

Like humanity in general, individual members of the RPA presented quite differently in one-to-one interactions such as being treated for wounds in the clinic or passing by in the street. The demeanour was then the diffidence of a shy young man instead of the belligerence when part of a group of comrades. We treated many of their wounds from the civil war, some of which had been untreated for 6 to 12 months. This presented some fascinating and difficult problems from the purely medical point of view. Our service helped to smooth relationships between us and they always expressed considerable gratitude, though they could be unreasonably demanding or critical of the final result. They appeared to have an idealised concept of the possible miracles of western medicine.

Their participation in the Kigali City to Surf also promoted understanding between the UN forces and the RPA.

The ADF medical services had minimal direct contact with hostile forces in East Timor but there was awareness of their presence and threat. Loaded weapons were the order of the day, particularly on the first deployment with INTERFET. It was a different story for the troopers out in the jungle who faced a constant threat from the 'militia' who had supported the Indonesian presence and then signalled their frustration with the decision for independence by killing innocent citizens and burning houses, businesses and public facilities. The danger was still there at the time of my third deployment and a New Zealand soldier was tragically murdered by the militia.

Insurgents and similar hostile groups made their presence felt in Iraq mainly by despatching ordnance such as rockets and mortar bombs onto the base or taking pot-shots at aircraft and the base with rifle fire. Suicide bombers attacked Iraqi workers queuing at the gate of the base on several occasions with terrible injuries. Generally, the attacks were remote and impersonal but we had face-to-face contact with one insurgent who was a suicide bomber. He survived after setting off his bomb and was taken to the operating theatre but his wounds were horrendous and he did not survive.

A number of the inpatients were insurgents who had been injured during combat and were being treated in the hospital such as a man who was shot in the knee while he was trying to set an IED. They were cocooned in security precautions and so we did not know much about them. They appeared just like any other Iraqi citizen but appeared more passive and did not say very much.

It was a similar situation in Afghanistan with the occasional inpatient being someone whose ambition in life was to kill those of us caring for him, though that did not inhibit demands for top quality care and attention while in hospital. A number of them were admitted after a premature explosion of homemade bombs that they were making. They squatted on the ground during the process and so they got a characteristic combination of blast injuries on the hands, in the face, on the inner aspect of the thighs and up into the groin. They gave imaginative reasons for the wounds in an attempt to explain away the obvious. A carrot exploded while being dug up, kicked by a goat, fell off a chair and fell asleep in front of the fire are a few of the samples.

Provision of ethical care in the hospital in Tarin Kowt was strict and this included not allowing inpatients to be interviewed or harassed by security agents, whether or not they were for or against us. This sometimes caused a bit of friction with the security agents but they usually waited until the suspect was discharged before pouncing on them. We were usually pleased to see the end of them because some appeared plainly evil.

Chapter 20
UN and NGO

My experiences with the United Nations (UN) have been negative. It is disappointing to think that an organisation that is responsible for the welfare of the world should be so uncaring and ineffectual. It is difficult to know where to start when discussing its deficiencies.

A good start would be to consider why countries such as Rwanda and East Timor got into a mess in the first place. Both have been victims of the UN's indecision and reticence to take action.

I found that the UN's support for its deploying personnel, military and civilian, was a story of cheapest options such as strange aircraft and crew for transport in and out of the deployment location and low priority for food and accommodation. Equipment and supplies were not always at a level that enabled tasks to be accomplished, such as bottles of oxygen and anaesthetic gases delivered empty. Some UN staff appeared more concerned with their own self-indulgent experiences and were frequently disrespectful to the local citizens.

The UN were niggardly in saving money by providing poor quality services and supplies and yet there was cavalier wastage of resources and equipment. In Rwanda, there were yards full of trashed four-wheel drive vehicles with UN on the doors in large letters. These were the ones that were not roadworthy. The ones that could move were driven around the streets of Kigali by the RPA. These vehicles had been coated with rough camouflage paint but it was still possible to see the UN letters showing through.

I was pleased that the command structures of my deployments were such that I was under the direct control of a commanding officer who answered directly to superiors in the ADF and not the UN. This meant that directions from above would be based on realism and not wishful thinking. I shudder to think of the Belgian soldiers in Rwanda whom the UN ordered to surrender their arms to a rioting mob and were then taken away to be tortured and murdered.

The only outfit that could make the UN look good was a Non-Government Organisation (NGO) and these appeared in droves if there was a chance of publicity such as television cameras. They were most visible at the time of the tsunami in PNG. They were all over the place during the early days when news coverage was at its peak but, when the media left, they faded from sight like moths disappearing when the light is turned off. Their first priority was the erection of tents and banners and this commitment was not hampered by the burden of actually getting out and doing the things they said that they were going to do.

A Japanese NGO had the largest banner and they were distressed when it mysteriously disappeared. Unsuccessfully searching for it became their main obsession though I am not sure this made much difference to their potential contribution.

A team of dog handlers appeared from the US with the intention of using their dogs to search for living victims but they were disappointed to learn that the six-day time lapse between the tsunami and their arrival meant that any victim lying injured in the jungle would be dead. Nonetheless, they ran around the camp with their dogs to get them ready for their mission and ventured out of the camp on a few occasions but I never heard whether they found anything. One of the dogs was a husky and had to be carried around because it could not function in the tropical heat and humidity. The handlers were particularly interested in our ADF T-shirts and requested swaps, presumably so that they could add the prize of our shirts to their T-shirt collection. They all expressed distress after a few days and left for Port Moresby for 'rest and recreation'.

NGOs began appearing in increasing numbers over the three deployments in East Timor and had similar characteristics but with some differences because they were longer in the country.

There were some troubling features about many of the workers in NGOs. Many were young men and women who could be described as 'bright eyed and bushy tailed'. Their expedition seemed to be an exciting adventure for their own fulfilment rather than to assist a distressed community. The local citizens became contemptuous when they perceived the disrespect and arrogance. This was most noticeable when the NGOs gave inexperienced young workers large four-wheel drive vehicles which they used to charge around with doubtful purpose except sightseeing. They regarded this as sufficiently important to harass the locals if they got in their way. Their main contribution to the recovery of the country was the boost to the economy of the country through their frequent restaurant meals and souvenir purchasing.

There were shining lights amongst the NGOs that compensated for the darkness of others.

The Salvation Army provided excellent support for local citizens and the deployed Australian forces in East Timor. The regular visit by their van with goods, some essential and some 'little' luxuries such as books and toiletries, was keenly anticipated. The driver and provider were always cheerful and usually had bits of gossip from around the country with news of activity in other camps and bases. I am not sure whether he added to truth or rumour but it was always good to speak to someone outside the ADF system and this tended to give him more credibility than higher sources in the ADF. The 'Sallies' did much pastoral work with the local East Timorese and were well received.

The ICRC was prominent in several of the deployments and was always professional. Their traditional role is the impartial management of battleground wounds regardless of the side and ideology of the casualty. This aspect was not visible to us as we were sequestered away in our own hospital which was unholy ground to the ICRC because of their commitment to no uniforms, no weapons, no military and no alliance with any of the combatants. They also undertook other roles, such as providing hospital care in the local hospital in East Timor and treating tsunami victims in PNG. This provided professional contact between health workers of a defence force and health workers of a high-level civilian NGO. It became apparent that there were more similarities than differences such as the priority to treat on clinical indications and not on the identity or alliances of the casualty. They shared our basic principles of battle-field surgery which is the removal of all contamination, thorough cleaning of the wound, leave the wound open and avoid metal fixation of broken bones. The surgery is simple and basic. The ethics and absence of self-glorification of the ICRC and its workers are appealing.

Another NGO with an ethos of providing a useful service and getting on with the job was Handicap International in Rwanda. This was an organisation that provided splints, crutches, artificial limbs, wheelchairs and suchlike for local victims of warlike injuries such as gunshot wounds and blast injuries from land mines. Even more importantly, they employed local craftsmen and taught them the skills of splint making. Many of the injured regained independence only with the assistance of Handicap International. They had one overseas orthotist from Belgium who was quiet and unassuming and several locals who were cheerful and enthusiastic about their work. In Iraq, lack of an orthotist who could provide these types of aids made rehabilitation of local amputees much more difficult.

I believe that Médicins sans Frontières (MSF) was present in all countries where I worked but I had no contact with them. They have a good reputation for dedication and quality of work.

Likewise, there were several good NGO aeromedical evacuation teams with medical staff and aircraft but we never made contact with them because the RAAF or the military of other countries fulfilled that role.

Chapter 21
Return Home

Returning home from a deployment is not simply a matter of packing your bag and hopping onto an aircraft. There are all sorts of issues and glitches waiting to prevent it going smoothly.

The first concern is whether they have arranged a replacement for you and, if so, whether he or she will arrive because, if not, you will be obliged to remain on the deployment until there is a replacement. The next concern is whether training and transport for the replacement have fallen into place and they actually arrive. I have been fortunate and the longest delay I have experienced has been two to three days.

Equipment such as weapons, ammunition, body armour, gas masks, special clothing, mosquito protection and sundry other items have to be handed back and checked against the list recorded on arrival. Every round of ammunition must be accounted for and there are fearsome repercussions if any is missing.

Personal and military equipment that is returning with you must be inspected by the Australian Quarantine and Inspection Service (AQIS) and this is sometimes done in the country of the deployment. This was the case in East Timor and the public servants were unfailingly cheerful, helpful but very, very thorough. Their interests were tiny seeds of Siam weed caught in Velcro strapping, mud on boots, nuts or wood being taken back as souvenirs, fruit, vegetables and, heaven forbid, reptiles or insects that had stowed away in echelon bags. This was quite a jolly and sociable event when it was done in a country where there was plenty of room and time.

It was done on arrival back in Australia on other occasions and it was just as thorough but not as much fun because it was at the end of a long trip and everyone was anxious to get back to their loved ones. The AQIS was always as helpful as possible but was always thorough and professional in their most important job of keeping Australia safe from unwanted plant and animal invaders.

I had a few goods confiscated. I bought an interesting boardgame in Rwanda that consisted of little wooden balls in a plank of wood with little hollows for the balls. A Rwandan tried to explain the game but without success. It transpired that the little wooden balls were actually seeds and so were confiscated but I could keep the wooden plank. I brought a huge shield back from PNG that unfortunately contained shells. Again, AQIS tried to be as helpful as possible and, rather than dispose of it, they took it away to have intensive fumigation but it fell apart and that was that.

One of my colleagues in Vanimo set a standard for wooden souvenirs that will never be surpassed. He was admiring a dugout canoe being paddled by some of the local residents and expressed his interest. After a lot of bargaining, he bought it in exchange for several ADF Rat-Packs. Apparently, it was a leaky old canoe that they were about to discard and so anything was a profit for the locals. The canoe was cleared by AQIS, packed onto the C-130 and ended up in Ingleburn Barracks in South-West Sydney. It was apparently left there forever though I guess something happened to it when Ingleburn was closed and all was transferred to Holsworthy Barracks.

We packed our bags after the AQIS inspection, which could be difficult if we were taking back more than we had on arrival. My habit was to only fill the backpack and webbing when arriving for the deployment and then carry them in the echelon bag. Personal goods could be split between the bags in the accommodation and then there was an extra bag for the trip home if necessary.

Hopefully, the replacement team had arrived by now and so a day was required to orientate them to the base and the situation. The accommodation was tight for a day or two while two teams were present and it was sometimes a question as to who should go into the temporary accommodation, the arriving or the departing.

'Return to Australia' psychological assessments were always compulsory. These were done on return to Australia after my earlier deployments and I took great pride in avoiding them. They were done in the country of the later deployments and you were not allowed to depart until that particular box was ticked. I had a few pleasant chit-chats with experts on human behaviour who were less than half my age.

There was often a little social 'hails and farewells' on the last night when the teams changed over. This could vary from amateur theatricals to nothing better than an early night in bed. Rwanda was a low-key affair because most of the higher ranks had been called to the UN commander's house for dinner. Eventually, we had a few drinks and speeches but then had to hang around to 1 o'clock in the morning waiting for our armed escort back to quarters. Nothing surpassed the Sing-Sing that preceded our departure from Vanimo PNG.

The day of departure was usually a glut of the military tradition of 'hurry up and wait'. If anything had been scheduled for a specific time, it was highly likely to be delayed and confuse all later schedules, though these often solved the problem by also being delayed. Steps that were at risk included: transport from the base, security clearances, transport to the departure lounge, boarding the aircraft and eventual take-off. Any and all of these stages could be delayed. The only time departures occurred on schedule was if you turned up one minute late, in which case you could watch your transport disappearing over the horizon.

There was always concern that the aircraft would not turn up to take us home and rumours flourished. In Rwanda, we were told by a 'reliable source' that all UN aircraft had been diverted to transport Ethiopian refugees and would not be available for days if not weeks. In Bougainville, we had to sit in an open paddock on 'Bob Marley's' property in the open for ages while we watched 'Bob Marley' till his soil with a hoe and waited interminably for the 'Herc' to turn up. Eventually, it arrived, did the two obligatory swoops over the runway to scare off humans and animals and then landed. The new medical team jumped out and we jumped in. No handover ceremony on this occasion.

There was a little more anxiety about the departure from Balad, Iraq, than other deployments because a British C-130 had crashed with no survivors about six weeks prior to our departure. There were many theories about the fate of the aircraft but most revolved around hostile actions by insurgents. Rumours put forward included a bomb planted on the aircraft, a lucky shot with small arms or RPG, a surface-to-air missile that uncharacteristically struck its target and then exploded, it hit the ground because it was flying too low, an on-board accident with weapon or cargo and so on. The only unthinkable possibility not considered was that the impregnable old workhorse had crashed because of a mechanical failure. We were visited by General Peter Cosgrove, then Chief of Defence Force, who raised the topic, presumably to give reassurance of our safety for the trip home. There was an impression that he was going to provide some inside information but, when he heard all of our own theories, he said that we seemed to know all about it and we never profited from his knowledge.

The actual departure from Balad typified the frustrations and dangers of the deployment to Iraq. We were scheduled to board our RAAF C-130 at 1500hrs and so we were required to check in all baggage the night before and leave our carry-on daypacks with the transport system at 0630. This left us with only the clothes that we stood up in, plus helmet, body armour and rifle, for about nine hours. Eventually, we kitted up in the helmets and armour and were deposited on the front apron of the tarmac at 1400 and waited for over an hour. We eventually heard the C-130 but could not see it because it was using the high altitude and rapid descent approach for protection from ground attack. Almost simultaneously, the 'red alert' siren sounded indicating that the base was being attacked by mortars or rockets. We were hustled off the tarmac and into the shelters where we sat for ages until the 'all clear' siren. One of the bombs or missiles had landed on the runway and so there was a further wait while they swept the runway to ensure that it was safe. Meanwhile, the 'Herc' kept circulating at high altitude while we wondered if it had enough fuel to stay indefinitely or whether it would go home and we would have to wait for another day. Eventually, it landed, we hopped on board and we took off at 1900 with us in body armour and rifles carefully pointed downwards so that, if we accidentally fired them, we would not put a round through the vital structures in the roof of the aircraft.

All of this was in complete contrast to the departure from Bali after my brief deployment after the second Bali bombing. We were delivered into the country by RAAF C-130. The aircraft had been immediately turned around to transport casualties back to Australia while we remained in Bali to treat any additional casualties who came out of the woodwork. There are diplomatic and protocol issues with military aircraft landing in a foreign country and so it was thought best that a C-130 not return to take us back home and we should travel on civilian aircraft. At this time we were keeping a low profile in a luxury hotel, wearing our camouflage uniforms and carrying equipment that made us look a bit warlike. There are diplomatic and protocol issues with military personnel wearing battle gear in a foreign country and so a person from the Australian Embassy was tasked with buying us some Bali-style shorts and tropical shirts so that we could get from the hotel to the airport. I can vaguely recall some hiccups in the check-in procedure but not the details. We also met many NGO and civilian AME teams going through the same procedure.

The ADF had been shunting personnel in and out of the Middle East for quite a few years by the time of my deployment to Afghanistan and so the procedures were much more structured and formal. This meant that there was much more that had to be done but at least it was done more efficiently and on schedule. The frustration of finding that the person who was vital for getting an essential step completed was on two weeks leave no longer occurred.

Getting out of Tarin Kowt and onto the aircraft travelling to Australia was a two-day procedure with a full schedule for each of the days. In Tarin Kowt, we had to pack bags, leave them for pick-up by 0630 and then assist in loading and unloading for their delivery to Movements, which is the name for military departure lounges. Movements were not yet opened and so computers, which were packed separately for protection, had to be taken back to accommodation and returned later. Then there was a Movements brief and luggage was opened and inspected for Dangerous Goods (DG). We then had to 'bomb up' by dressing in body armour, helmets and rifles and were transported to the runway. The C-130 was on schedule on this occasion and it is a dramatic sight landing in Tarin Kowt because the runway is unsealed and there are huge clouds of red dust in the trail of the aircraft. We were taken to the ADF base in Kuwait where we packed and handed in body armour and special winter clothing that we never needed to wear. We checked in weapons and our ammunition was counted to ensure we had not used any. We filled out forms for the psychologist, got pay information, we were instructed about luggage by Movements (again), luggage was inspected by AQIS, we had a psychology de-brief and then we went to 'Fat Alley' for a monster pizza at Pizza Hut. We stayed overnight and left for Sydney on a charter flight the next day.

The return home is a mixture of emotions. You get on the aircraft in a war zone and get off in the artificial modern civilisation of an international airport. The arrival in the deployment zone can be confusing and the return equally so because of the dramatic contrast in the environment. There can be relief that there is a safe return. There can be a feeling of anti-climax that the thrills of the deployment are now over and it is back to mundane normality. Loved ones are waiting and welcoming. It is wonderful to be reunited but there can be an element of caution in case one or other has changed over the course of the deployment. There is a desire to share experiences but there is uncertainty whether others will really understand what occurred.

There is a wish to rest and catch your breath for a few weeks after a deployment but, unfortunately, this was a therapy that was never practical for me at the end of my deployments. I was an orthopaedic surgeon in a sole practice and the only funds that the practice earned were from my own efforts. These efforts had ceased for the duration of the deployment and the practice was not earning income. Meanwhile, the expenses such as staff, insurance and office continued. There is a lag time of about six weeks from the treatment of a patient to payment and so this meant that funds were coming in while I was on deployment but then dried up just as I arrived home because I had done no work for six weeks or more. There was no current income for the practice and so I had to get straight back to work to keep the practice solvent. This was often a hard time when I had not fully re-adjusted on return from deployment but had to immediately start my normal work at full speed.

The deployment could also affect patient attitudes. Some were impressed that 'their' doctor had undertaken such an adventure. Others were unimpressed that 'their' doctor was not available when they needed him. I probably lost more patients from my practice than I gained when I deployed. I sympathise with them. If you need your doctor, you want him now and reasons for lack of availability, no matter how noble, are judged unacceptable.

Referrals from general practitioners followed a similar pattern. Most were supportive and some made a point of increasing referrals on my return to help the practice. Some were frustrated at my absence and shifted their referrals elsewhere, some even describing me as too often "on holiday" as the reason for removing support. On balance, general practitioners provided much more support than rejection. Presentations on the deployment and similar public relation efforts could restore visibility to the referral base, though one ADF surgeon colleague triggered complaints of unethical self-promotion from his jealous colleagues when he simply gave an invited speech at a conference regarding his deployment to the Middle East.

One of the first things that hit me when I returned to my routine practice was the contrast between the mundane treatment of commonplace orthopaedic conditions and the drama of military surgery. It was difficult to get into perspective complaints of sore big toes or a knee that was painful when sitting in a cinema. All diseases, injuries and complaints are important to the sufferer and the surgeon must take them seriously and do the best to help. I could find this a little difficult for the first few weeks when my mind was still on the soldier with both legs blown off by an IED or the child who had stepped on a landmine. There was not much to be done except wait for adaptation back to routine practice.

I found it difficult to talk about my experiences, even with immediate family and close friends. The interaction between people is frequently sharing of related experiences when a social group with common interests meet for talking, dining, partying, meeting in homes and all other socialising. My experiences were singular and had not been experienced by my social group and so responses were not on the same wavelength. Some people could not relate to my stories because they had never had similar experiences and were frustrated or resentful that they could not respond with a similar or better story. Usually, they terminated the conversation very early and I imagined rolling of eyes and the unspoken comment, "Here he goes again." Others would respond with the comment that they already knew all about it because of an event that they had previously experienced which they would describe but it was usually something that I found not comparable and I would feel diminished that my experiences were reduced to a lower level. This would make me feel bad and I would wonder whether I had misconceptions about the deployments. It became easier not to talk about it at all.

On several occasions, I surprised myself by becoming tearful which was enormously embarrassing. I was being interviewed by a journalist for a suburban paper about my experiences in Iraq and was happily enjoying sharing the experiences with someone who was keen to get information, even though it was on a professional level. She asked, 'What was my worst experience in Iraq?' I immediately answered, as if a reflex, 'I would be happy if I never again saw someone whose legs have been blown off,' and then burst into tears. I am still unsure how I went so quickly from cheerful to tearful. Another occasion was when discussing the deployments with casual acquaintances in a tourist resort and I became tearful while describing the Kibeho massacre in Rwanda, even though it was not one of my personal experiences. There were other similar occasions but it has not been a frequent event.

I do not believe that I have had any of the mental issues that have tormented many of those who have recently deployed, though the 'shrinks' may interpret this as dangerous self-delusion. I think that there are a number of reasons why my psyche has not been left with permanent scars. I am mature aged and so had realistic expectations and had already experienced the rough and smooth of life. My profession as a surgeon had already hardened me to the sights and horrors of major wounds, distressed humans and death. I am a Reservist and could escape from the clutches of the ADF immediately on return to Australia. I believe the statistics are that full-time service personnel have more problems than Reservists on return home. I had to immediately return to my full-time profession because of financial requirements and this diverted me from dwelling on the past. There was good family support.

The Return to Australia (RTA) reception for a mature Reservist may differ from a young full-time ADF member. I heard several stories of younger full-time ADF members who experienced some resentment and jealousy from colleagues from the time that they were identified for deployment and continuing well after their RTA. I was told by a number of full-timers that they got messages such as, 'why did they pick you to go, I am just as good as you', 'we had to work harder while you were away', 'now you are back, you can catch up on all of the work that you left behind', 'you do not deserve to have special leave just because you were deployed' and 'I do not want to hear all of your stories about being a hero on deployment'. This could occur while they were at their most stressed and vulnerable immediately on return and they could feel lonely and rejected just when they needed support. There are also other factors why the bad mental effects of a deployment can linger for many years.

Personally, I always felt unsettled for weeks or months after a deployment and I usually made up my mind that I would never do it again. All multi-faceted events have positives and negatives and I gradually forgot the bad and remembered the good. I would become restless, desire a repeat of the excitement and anticipate the next opportunity to deploy. Now my deploying career has finished but it remains strong in my memory and I miss it.

Chapter 22
Reflections

Arrival on deployment in a war zone immediately reveals big differences between military surgery and surgery in a civilian setting. It is said that "truth is the first casualty of war" but ethics are also at risk. The deployed military surgeon faces ethical dilemmas that are more complex and not as easy to resolve as they are in a civilian setting.

The first dilemma is the need to provide service to two masters, the patient and the command structure of the deployed forces. Whether in the military or civilian setting, a doctor's duty is to do the best for the sick or injured patient who has presented for treatment. This is the universal expectation of the doctor-patient relationship. In civilian practice, it is not unusual for the doctor to act as an advocate for the patient when tackling bodies such as insurance companies, government bodies and employers. Confidentiality is paramount with no release of information unless the patient gives permission.

The situation in the military, particularly on deployment, is not quite as simple. The ADF recruits and posts Medical Officers to provide the best possible medical treatment for their serving members. Every member of a deployed team has vital responsibilities and it is important to the entire team that all remain functioning. Consequently, the command team want to know if health issues are causing one of their team to weaken and the expectation is that the MO will always keep the CO informed if a health issue is likely to blunt the sharp end of the deployment. This would be a clear breach of confidentiality in civilian medicine but it is necessary in the military setting where life and death for many might hang on the healthy capability of a vital person. ADF members know that lack of confidentiality exists and are informed of this at the time of recruitment. Sailors, soldiers and airmen sign away many personal freedoms when they are recruited into the ADF. This is universal for all defence forces. In Iraq, we operated on US defence force personnel without obtaining signed consent. We explained verbally to those who were conscious and, for those who were comatose from injuries or from heavy sedation, we just "got on with it".

Doctors are taught from the earliest days of medical school that treatment is provided according to the need of the patient and priority is given to the patients whose need is greatest. Generally, these principles hold well in civilian medicine but can be distorted by economics and the capability of the treating facility. The situation in the military is more complex and the military surgeon can be confronted with ethical dilemmas that sit uneasily with usual values. A few examples follow.

If resources are swamped by mass casualties, the principle is to do maximum good for the maximum number of casualties with the available resources. Delaying treatment for minor or non-life-threatening injuries is logical. More difficult is the decision about a seriously injured casualty with life-threatening injuries and with a slim chance of surviving but will require total care by many personnel and much equipment to the extent that other casualties with less severe injuries may be neglected resulting in severe disability or death. The hard decision may be that the most serious injury is neglected so that a larger number of casualties can be given a chance of survival.

The purpose of health personnel on deployment is to care for the health of deployed ADF members and this takes priority over most other matters including treatment of local civilians. It can be said that the treatment is discriminatory in favour of military personnel to the detriment of civilians. It becomes more complicated if a local dignitary or influential 'VIP' has medical problems because then pressure is put on the administrators of the deployment to provide treatment, sometimes in preference to deployed military personnel and certainly in preference to less privileged local civilians. Maintaining the support of the VIP may be vital for the success of the mission and it is politic to consent to the request. The end result is that there are different levels of access to the military medical facilities which is an acknowledgement of pragmatic reality in the battlefield but does not match the ethics expected in civilian practice. This can vex civilian surgeons who are deployed to a war zone.

Supply lines to a medical facility in an insecure combat zone are limited and re-supply is not guaranteed. Resources must be conserved to ensure there are the tools required when the need arises. This can mean rationing treatment to local civilians or using an alternative treatment that does not drain resources. The best solution is to get the local health service up and running so that local civilians do not seek out the military hospital.

The health facility must provide support for front-line combat troops heading for the battleground and at risk of wounding if they make contact with the enemy. This means having personnel, equipment, supplies, empty hospital beds, resuscitation and operating theatre all available for possible battleground casualties. All other work is restricted at this time, no matter the urgency of the case or the importance of the patient so that resources are available.

The combination of local dignitaries insisting on being treated by military staff, the need to ration resources, avoidance of becoming the *de facto* local health service and the task of providing support for ADF members expecting to make contact with the enemy means that many of the decisions regarding treatment and allocation of resources are made by non-medical commanders and administrators who have no concern about the ethics of treatment allocation. This has led to clashes between health workers and administrative personnel. For example, in Rwanda, there were discussions as to whether external fixation equipment for broken bones could be used on Rwandans or only on deployed military personnel.

In East Timor, Iraq and Afghanistan, we sometimes treated detainees who were suspected insurgents. Many were violent and murderous. They wished us harm and ethical treatment was difficult. They were isolated from other patients, guarded, sometimes handcuffed and were generally sullen and surprisingly demanding and uncooperative with treatment provided. Nonetheless, they were treated as well as possible. Interrogation was not allowed in hospital but the security people always jumped on them quickly after their discharge from the hospital.

A vivid memory of my deployment to Iraq was an incident when a suicide bomber blew himself up along with many other people waiting at the gates of Balad. The bomber had not died immediately and was brought into the hospital for emergency care but did not survive for long. I can recall looking at him amongst the ghastly wounds of the victims and wondering what sort of lunatic would do such a thing.

A few years later, I visited the ICRC Museum in Geneva and bought a book entitled *What Terrorists Want* in search of answers to some of my questions about terrorists in general and suicide bombers in particular. I was amazed to read that suicide bombers are not psychiatrically disturbed or even psychologically abnormal. They have certain personality characteristics but are rational and their actions are logical once their motivation is understood. They come from many different backgrounds. Some are young, some are old, some have no education, some have a university education, some are single, some are married with children, women and men are involved, and pregnant women have been bombers. There is no consistent pattern.

This surprising knowledge stimulated an urge to learn more and so I did some considerable background reading and started a university diploma course for a short period of time. Terrorism is a fascinating area of study because it covers such a wide spectrum of humanity and inhumanity. Topics include definitions of terrorism, history, religion, politics, geography, economics, training, communication, psychology, military tactics, future events, gender differences, links with criminal organisations and many more surprising aspects of an ugly facet of the human race.

I have found ANZAC Day a difficult time since my deployments. The Australian and New Zealand Army Corps (ANZAC) were part of the tragic sea borne invasion of Gallipoli, Turkey, on 25 April 1915 and the date has been embedded in the history of both countries. Now 25 April is ANZAC Day which is the traditional day to acknowledge and remember military service and sacrifice by sailors, soldiers and airmen in Australia. I am proud of my service and the medals that have been awarded but have been uneasy about displaying them in public, even though it is natural and comfortable to display them in company with other serving and retired members of the ADF. This is due to my perception that my service does not measure up to the hardships and dangers of those who served in the two World Wars, Korea and Vietnam and I sense pretension within myself. I avoided marching on ANZAC Day for many years but have done so for the past few years and have met many of the veterans from previous conflicts and so have been able to judge their reaction to someone such as myself joining their march.

The first message that I got from a World War II veteran was when I was invited to a RAAF Association dinner. (The RAAF Association is a social network for serving and retired RAAF members of all ranks. It has no connection with the ADF.) An old gentleman with an equally old RAAF uniform fitted with Squadron Leader rank, strings of medals and pilot's wings introduced himself and asked about my military service. I provided a brief history, returned the question and was treated with a fascinating account of his service flying in New Guinea and other areas of the South Pacific during World War II. He casually described hair-raising events typified by near disaster, narrow escapes and triumphant raids. It sounded like something from a *Boys' Own Adventures* story. I told him how my experiences paled alongside his and he responded with warm praise and reassurance that my experience compared favourably with most veterans marching on ANZAC Day. He then made a point that had not occurred to me but subsequently altered my attitude to my participation in the march. He expressed concern that he was getting old and all of his comrades were getting old and soon none of them would be left to keep the march going. He emphasised how it was important for my generation of returned servicemen to participate so that the tradition never died out. This stirred me to commence marching and I have not missed marching somewhere on ANZAC Day since 2014. My justification is that I am not marching for myself but I am marching for the memory of all servicemen who have gone before me and did not return or have returned but are no longer able to participate.

A number of veterans have repeated this sequence of welcome, interest in my own service, description of extreme service and then encouragement to 'keep the flag flying'. Veterans' biggest fear is that ANZAC Day will slowly fade away as numbers dwindle and they will be forgotten. They can remember how the day was disrespected and became diminished during the 1960s and 1970s.

Black humour occurs in confronting, frightening and tragic situations and so it is endemic in both the military and the medical professions. Combine the two during a health deployment into a war-like situation and black humour is inevitable. It is debatable whether it should have exposure in this book but it would be remiss to censor it from a 'warts and all' description of deployment.

Three examples spring to mind that are marginally printable. All other examples that spring to mind are unprintable.

One of my colleagues in Rwanda could not resist the temptation to rename some of our patients. He named two women with amputations of single legs 'Eileen' and 'Lena'. The boy with bilateral amputations was called 'Neil'. A woman with an amputation and bladder injury requiring a catheter was called 'Kathleen'.

Confession! I am not without guilt. I was repairing an injured finger on a young boy in East Timor when the concerned theatre nurse asked me whether he would keep the finger. I could not resist the temptation to tell her that, "Yes, he will as long as he puts it in a bottle and keeps it in the fridge." Fortunately, his finger healed well and remained on his hand and I am not sure whether this removes the comment from the definition of black humour.

One of our mass casualties in Balad, Iraq, occurred when a car bomb detonated near a bus full of Iraqi soldiers. Apparently, they were lulled into a false sense of security because the car was occupied by a man and a woman. This triggered interesting theories amongst the US such as one of the occupants was a trainee suicide bomber and the other was an experienced suicide instructor. It was also postulated that the true suicide bomber was unable to drive or read maps and so they had to hire a professional driver or navigator to complete the mission. The facetious theory that the woman could not be allowed out alone for religious reasons may have been closer to the truth than realised. The most likely explanation is that it was for tactical reasons and the deception successfully got them under the security screen. The theories expanded when another suicide vehicle had no less than four occupants. It was suggested that there were not enough vehicles and so some had to get a lift or it was a car-sharing scheme to cut down on traffic congestion and pollution.

Black humour has been defined as a form of humour that regards human suffering as absurd rather than pitiable, or that considers human existence as ironic and pointless but somehow comic. Psychological explanations of black humour are along the lines of making sense of distressing situations and coping with the stress, but I am not sure whether this is simply a justification for bad behaviour.

Water and sanitary carts used by the Australian Imperial Forces in World War 1 were manufactured by the Furphy foundry in Shepparton, Victoria, and had the name 'Furphy' painted on in large letters. The end plate also had cast sayings and truisms, the best-known being:

Good, better, best
Never let it rest
Till your good is better
And your better is best

The carts were a popular gathering point for thirsty soldiers who would gossip and exchange false rumours dressed as fact. These were called a 'Furphy'. On my deployments, the Furphy water cart had been replaced by plastic bottles of water but the false rumours were still alive and kicking. Many of the rumours revolved around transport out and usually consisted of pessimism about the likely non-availability of aircraft.

Rwanda was a fertile field of rumours. There was one that someone had bought an AK47 from an RPA soldier, had dismantled it and was posting it home bit by bit. He had almost succeeded but was caught when he attempted to post the butt.

There was another that a soldier had been caught by an RPA officer while he was in bed with his wife. He rapidly departed out of a window and took the RPA officer's rifle as a precaution. He was court-martialled by the ADF but the case was unsuccessful because, when they asked that the RPA officer give evidence, they were told that he had been executed for losing his weapon.

The mysterious Middle East would not be mysterious without 'true' stories. The downing of the RAF Hercules in Iraq initiated many rumours, some realistic and some fanciful. The most outlandish was that it had been hijacked by Al Qaeda.

It was rumoured that the heavily armed Marine who counted the numbers of customers entering the mess in Balad was clicking up exorbitant amounts of money for some friend of George W Bush. In Vanimo, PNG, it was rumoured that we were accompanied by Special Forces hidden in our midst and armed to the teeth for our security. The Afghan guards in Tarin Kowt also stirred the rumour mill. They were all Taliban. Their machine guns were pointing into the compound and not out of it. Several jumped the wall and deserted to the insurgents every night.

Chapter 23
A Reservist's Perspective of the Australian Defence Force

The Commanding Officer (CO) of a deployment is the key to its success and dictates the satisfaction and achievement of the deployed personnel. A deployment that has a struggling CO tends to be unhappy while a well-organised and successful deployment guided by a good CO is satisfying even if the workload is onerous.

By and large, I was fortunate that the COs of my deployments were supportive and gifted with common sense. They could perform the difficult balancing act of maintaining morale and a sense of well-being by keeping the team focussed and functioning during the inevitable difficult times. This also required team members to toughen up and pull their weight when the orders came. Prima donnas cause problems out of proportion to their importance on a deployment.

It was interesting to experience the difference between Army and RAAF COs. Using the carrot and stick analogy, Army COs tended towards stick and RAAF COs tended towards carrot. There is a place for both approaches at times but personally, I was more comfortable with the RAAF carrot, probably because I was a member of the RAAF and was familiar with their methods.

The task for the CO could become difficult because of rank inversion. My rank rose from Squadron Leader (Major equivalent) to Wing Commander (Lieutenant Colonel equivalent) to Group Captain (Colonel equivalent) over the course of my deployments and most times I held a higher rank than the CO. Most of my fellow specialists held a similar rank and so it was not unusual for the CO to be out-ranked by quite a number of the personnel who were under his command. The military protocols for the chain of command are clear. The authorisation to give orders and the obligation to obey are a factor of the respective appointments of the individuals and not the rank. An extreme example could be the Chief of Defence Force (CDF) travelling in a C-130 flown by a Flight Lieutenant. The CDF may have given the orders for the strategic task of the C-130 but once it is in the air the pilot is responsible for the success of the flight and the safety of occupants and so has control of the behaviour of passengers and crew and can give orders accordingly. The CDF must obey if the pilot gives orders regarding safety, weapon security and everything else that aircrew instruct passengers.

Medical specialists' tasks on deployment are usually limited to their medical speciality with some additional tasks added to the general support of the deployment. Any command roles are limited and subordinate to the command of the CO. This is an extremely important principle for specialists to follow otherwise the authority of the CO is undermined. Unfortunately, on a few occasions, some specialists attempted to 'pull rank' on the CO. This created difficulties such as embarrassment and bother for the CO as he compelled correct behaviour by the miscreant, unwarranted resentment by the specialist with potential for further conflict and the creation of an impression that medical specialists are prima donnas who throw their weight around. The only comfort for non-specialists was the demeaning spectacle of two specialists trying to pull rank on each other such as an anaesthetist who out-ranked a surgeon trying to order the surgeon how to do surgery or a surgeon who out-ranked an anaesthetist trying to order the anaesthetist how to give an anaesthetic.

I cannot recall ever being exclusively under medical command. I was always deployed in a health unit with an officer with a health background as CO but there was always a further chain of command reaching upwards into high ranked officers who were responsible for all facets of the deployment including the health unit. Their background was operational command and often with a combat connection such as infantry or logistics but certainly not health. Sometimes this resulted in the health unit being required to take a role directed by non-medical people who looked at the issues with different eyes from the health personnel, including the CO. At times it was almost a clash of cultures and the CO of the health unit could be the meat in the sandwich between a superior officer who was ordering a certain action and the medical staff who were saying the action was not good medicine or possibly unethical.

Another quirk of the command structure arose when I deployed to Iraq and again in Afghanistan. In Iraq, I deployed with an Australian Medical Detachment that was under the command of a RAAF Nursing Officer who was under the command of the non-medical Australian overall commander of the ADF forces in the Middle East. We were located on a large USAF Base in Balad and so we were under the control of the USAF commandant of the base. The hospital was also USAF and the CO of the hospital was a USAF officer with full control of the hospital and was responsible for the policies that affected my medical activities such as surgical options and treatment of patients. This supervision and direction of my surgery were delegated downwards to the head of surgery in the unit who was a USAF surgeon. This adds up to five different levels of command that were heading in my direction but it worked well because problems had been anticipated and the protocols had been formed in advance. The key was that the Australian command structure was separate from the US structure. We worked with them, we respected their authority in their facilities and we cooperated with their objectives, which was easy to do because we were on the same wavelength. However, we had retained sufficient independence to protect ourselves from being coerced into actions that were not compatible with ADF doctrine and principles.

The situation was similar in Tarin Kowt, Afghanistan. We were under the command of a RAAF Nursing Officer who, in turn, was under the command of ADF senior officers in the Middle East. We were seconded to a hospital owned and commanded by the Netherlands defence force and so we were obliged to follow the directions of the Dutch CO but had the option of appealing to the ADF hierarchy if the directions were unacceptable. Once again, we were all on the same wavelength and so there was never any incident of serious disagreement. The ADF was responsible for our movement and well-being while the Dutch were responsible for our tasks for the deployment. This deployment was a little more complex from my perspective because I was appointed Clinical Director and so had some responsibility for the day-to-day running of the hospital.

One of the most enjoyable aspects of a deployment with the ADF is being part of a supportive team with all members wishing each other success in their tasks and assisting each other to achieve their aims. There is no need for competition between doctors or with other health workers. The staff sits and waits and then deals with the sick and injured as they come through the front door. The de-brief on the end result is practical and helpful, no matter whether the result is successful or disappointing.

This contrasts with a civilian practice which is more competitive between health practitioners, both between individuals with the same speciality such as two surgeons, between different specialities such as anaesthetist and surgeon and between different professions such as doctors and nurses. This tendency to a slightly adversarial relationship leads to more stress and tension and can reduce the effectiveness of the overall management in a health facility.

It is the difference between everyone pulling together in the same direction and everyone pulling in different directions. The whole can be greater or less than the sum of the components, influenced by the degree of cooperation between individuals and departments. It is fortunate that military deployments usually achieve mutual support because there is no margin for error with limited staff and resources. A deployed military facility could not succeed if it were run as inefficiently as a civilian public hospital.

Deployed ADF medical units aim for an efficient worksite with cooperation and support between members but inefficient inter-service rivalry can counteract this.

I became aware of this on my first deployment to Rwanda when I was not sure if I was being over-sensitive or whether I was really being treated as a slightly lesser person because I was RAAF and not Army. My perception was confirmed when I was in conversation with two young RAAF NOs and I mentioned that I sometimes felt that my rank fell between the Army ranks. I was ranked Wing Commander which was equivalent to Lieutenant Colonel in the Army but I always felt that Army saw me as not reaching that level but did concede that I was higher than the next rank down which was Major. I was surprised by the strength of the agreement from the RAAF NOs who expressed considerable frustration that they did not get respect for their rank and qualifications from Army personnel and they believed it was making their job more difficult. They were permanent RAAF members and so the attitude from superiors was much more important for them than for a Reservist such as myself. For me, it was an amusing quirk that I would be rid of once the deployment finished but the RAAF NOs had a legitimate concern that the attitude could affect their future career prospects with the RAAF, particularly if their Army superiors were consistent with their misconception of RAAF personnel by putting in a negative report after the deployment.

There have been similar irritations on other deployments, particularly those which have been under Army command. This could include irritants such as not being included in decision making discussions, less respect for clinical opinion of RAAF personnel, fewer opportunities for trips outside the base, setting higher standards for weapon training because it is assumed that 'RAAF do not know how to do it' and other similar petty annoyances. It was nothing major but it was enough to reduce efficiency. It was easier for me as a high-ranking Reservist but it was no joke for junior officers and other ranks who were part of the permanent service and could be fearful that a bad report from an army commander, who was prejudiced about the RAAF, could affect their future career.

None of my deployments matched the predictions prior to departure. The wisdom of the ADF powers in Australia did not match the reality of the situation in the location of the deployment. I assumed that feedback from the deployment would be welcomed so that those deployed in the future could be put on the right track. This was not the case and I became accustomed to a lack of interest in any form of written or spoken report on return. Nonetheless, I felt it was important and so persisted with writing a summary of my 'lessons learnt' and gave presentations at conferences and seminars as often as possible. The areas that I thought could benefit from a user's feedback could be divided into military and medical. The military aspects were training, personal fitness and health, how to use personal and military equipment with maximum efficiency, command structures, relationships with other personnel and travel. Medical aspects were realistic expectations of treatment in an austere environment, how to make maximum use of restricted facilities and medical supplies, triage, matching treatment with the character of the patient, making allowances for limitations of aftercare on the departure of the military health team and need for better imaging and laboratory equipment.

I am not sure why there was lack of interest at all levels of ADF and Defence Department personnel, high ranks, low ranks, health and non-health. Possibly, they felt that they had done the research, got the information, already knew it all and did not have to be told differently by someone else, particularly a Reservist RAAF doctor. Possibly the decisions had been made and the system was too inflexible to make any changes and so it would be best to avoid nuisance information. Possibly, it was felt that the organisers and controllers in Australia had the big picture and those deployed only had a snapshot of one small area at a short instant of time. Possibly, there was an annoyance about someone who had had the excitement of a deployment and now had come back to 'criticise' the people who were stuck at home doing their best for them.

Whatever the reasons, I believe it is a pity that the opportunity was not taken to get maximum information from every person who had deployed so that errors could be corrected and the good things enhanced for the benefit of those deploying in the future. I was partly amused and partly distressed to attend a talk by an anaesthetist who had deployed to the Middle East nine years after my last deployment to Afghanistan. He presented a list of problems and complaints about training, RAAF versus Army, clothing, equipment, logistics, treatment decisions, personal health and accommodation that echoed all that many of us had been saying for years and had been trying to deliver the message on return to Australia. There have been similar reports of lack of availability and lack of training for the specialists who are currently required in the Middle East. I have attended seminars entitled 'Lessons Learnt' but it appears that not many lessons have been learnt.

The same disinterest in taking advantage of lessons learnt on military deployments also exists in the civilian world of orthopaedics. I wrote a paper on my experience in Balad with documentation of the battlefield injuries and the treatments performed because it was relevant to the occasional blast injuries that occur in civilian practice and would be particularly relevant treating mass casualties when an inevitable terrorist attack occurs in Australia. The intention was to present the information at the major conference of the Australian Orthopaedic Association but it was rejected as 'not relevant' and I was only invited to make the presentation on the intervention of an Army Reserve colleague. The presentation ended up in a side room at a dead period of the conference and few people attended. The first Bali bombing occurred a few months later and the comments that I have heard confirm my opinion that the treating surgeons would have been better informed if they had tapped into the experience of military orthopaedic surgeons who had previously treated battlefield blast injuries.

I was only a RAAF Reservist on deployment for short periods of time. The rest of the time I was a civilian orthopaedic surgeon in private practice and needing to earn an income to cover expenses for myself and my family. Practice expenses such as rent, salaries, insurance, registration and administration continued in my absence and meanwhile my income dropped substantially and the people who referred me patients were likely to forget about me. My RAAF payment stopped as soon as I got back to Australia and practice income had fizzled out. The expenses continued but I would have no income for two or three months while the practice got back on its feet.

One way to accelerate the return to the normal speed of the practice was to exploit the adventures of the deployment to get visibility with referring colleagues, particularly general practitioners. I would start this process before the deployment by sending out letters to referring doctors giving basic details of the deployment to avoid the misconception that I was leaving on prolonged recreational leave. I would send regular letters about the deployment 'from the front line', send a further letter once I had returned and then give as many talks and presentations to medical meetings as possible. Nonetheless, I would still have general practitioners and patients making critical comments about my unavailability during my 'long holiday'.

My longest deployment was to Balad, Iraq, which also provided the best opportunity for self-publicity. Heidi Miranda was a physiotherapist who owned a practice next door to my professional rooms in Castle Hill and we had a wonderful symbiotic professional relationship. For example, she introduced me to Eastwood District Rugby Football Club and I was their club doctor for a number of enjoyable years highlighted by sharing in their first Shute Shield premiership in 1999. Heidi's brother, Charles Miranda, was a senior journalist with *The Daily Telegraph* in Sydney. He wrote a sympathetic article about my deployment to Iraq and suggested that I send back regular articles while deployed which I agreed to do after I cleared the security issues with the appropriate people in the RAAF and the ADF.

Writing the articles was both enjoyable and educational. I was limited to 500 words for each article and I learnt the discipline of getting rid of unnecessary words. The articles are reproduced in the appendix of this book. Getting the articles back to Charles was a different matter. They had to be security-cleared by all commanders in the Middle East, who were my immediate CO in Balad, the overall ADF commander 'somewhere in the Middle East', the USAF CO of the hospital in Balad and then the USAF Commandant in Balad. All were complimentary about the articles and approved their publication. They were then sent to the public relations people in RAAF HQ in Springwood NSW who, we were assured, were salivating for good material to put a positive spin on RAAF activities in the Middle

East and it was their task to send the articles to Charles. All went well except that I kept getting a stream of increasingly impatient emails from Charles asking why I was not sending the requested articles. We eventually learnt that the articles had not shifted from the desk of timid PR people in Springwood who were afraid of either a "yes" or "no" decision and so had taken the easy step of making no decision at all. Eventually they were released for publication but in condensed form.

The irony was that we were visited by General Peter Cosgrove, CDF, during the deployment and he strongly encouraged us to get publicity for our service in Iraq because it shone a favourable light on the ADF. He appeared perplexed when told of the problems getting my articles cleared for publication.

Epilogue

Too many ADF personnel who return from a modern deployment come back with Post-Traumatic Stress Disorder (PTSD). I am not a psychologist or psychiatrist but I have attended courses where the topic has been discussed. One-third recovers, one-third improves and copes with the disorder and one-third never recovers and is permanently disabled. Apparently, we all have a level where we can cope with ghastly experiences but we decompensate into PTSD when that level is exceeded. I do not know if there are separate statistics for health workers such as doctors, nurses and medics but my impression is that my profession is less frequently affected. Our choice of profession may mean that we have self-selected into work that is more confronting because we sense our characters are more resistant. We may have become immune or tolerant of the horrors of war because of previous experiences in our civilian work.

I have now retired from surgical practice but continue consulting. I mainly provide medico-legal opinions and this includes assessment of discharged members of the ADF on behalf of the Australian Department of Veterans Affairs (DVA). My role is to assess their musculo-skeletal injuries but I have been distressed at the number of ADF veterans who have psychological issues that are apparent even to an orthopaedic surgeon. Some have lost home, family and finances and are living on the street. Some are only coping with the devoted support of long-suffering spouses and parents. Most have had problems shifting from the close-knit comradely support of the ADF into the DVA which they perceive as adversarial. This perception is reality for too many cases. Like many large organisations, public and private, the upper hierarchy of the DVA express the best of intentions but those who work with beneficiaries do not always practice what their superiors preach. Government support can easily miss the citizens being targeted and end up in the possession of those who know how to play the system. I have seen ex-servicemen needing support missing out completely while others with minimal problems have received disproportional benefits. I am pessimistic that this paradox will ever be resolved. Flexibility may be necessary and some get more than they deserve so that the most entitled get their share. This is not helped by the clashes between professions that must deal with reality and professions that deal in wishful thinking.

Why did I call this book "Sad Joys on Deployment"?

Whenever he was asked about his experiences while deployed to Balad, an Army surgical colleague always answered 'I had a ball'. I always felt some discomfort when hearing this response because it clashed with the human misery linked to the deployment. It was like the rider of a motorbike experiencing the thrill and excitement of the ride while his pillion seat passenger is terrified and miserable. Yet if I fairly analyse my inner reactions to the deployment, I need to use similar terms. Perhaps I 'had a ball' on all my deployments despite the dead, the wounded, the hatreds, the broken communities, the destroyed buildings and all the confronting scenes and situations.

How could this paradox have occurred?

Possibly, it was the civilian surgical training and experience. My career has been forty-five years of exposure to open wounds and broken bones, though not in the league and number like those found on a military deployment. Surgical training points the surgeon to 'fixing the problem' and avoiding an emotional reaction as it can cloud judgement of the best treatment option. Should a surgeon 'depersonalise' the casualty so that decisions are detached? Objective and not subjective? I enjoy my work as an orthopaedic surgeon and perhaps the surgical challenges of the deployments were the pinnacle of problems and the solutions were the pinnacle of surgical enjoyment. Nonetheless, it is important to maintain human connection with the casualty.

Possibly, it was the military training. I had attended classroom and practical courses. I had been trained how to handle a rifle and pistol and I had cupboards full of military equipment. I knew how to modify my surgical skills to combat wounds and mass casualties. There was excitement in putting this training into practice.

Possibly, it was my sense of personal fulfilment similar to the UN and NGO workers who expected local civilians to jump out of the way of their four-wheel drive vehicles and persuaded each other that their value was above the ordinary. Did the deployments provide something lacking in the rest of my life?

Whatever the reason, I came out of all the deployments with a positive sense of enjoyment. Yet I cannot reflect on each of them without being aware of the people who suffered, those whose circumstances had spiralled down out of their control and the visibility of the worst aspects of the human species. I cannot admit to enjoyment without being aware of the sadness of those who suffered.

Yet there were events that were happy and enjoyable, such as comradeship, military tourism, local cultural exchanges, that could push the tragedy and ugliness to the back of the mind. Joys were diminished by sadness and sadness was diminished by joys.

These conflicting emotions are not unique. I cannot express it any better than Pierre-Irénée Jacob, a pharmacist who spent many years in Napoleon's Grande Armée. On 3 October 1812 he wrote the following while he was marching to Russia:

> ...je faisais des réflexions bien sérieuses sur cette singulière manière de voyager à l'armèe. Cesser d'être son guide e son arbitre, en quelque sorte cesser d'être homme ; marcher ou s'arrêter, selon la volonté d'une puissance invisible qui vous dirige ; telle est la condition de la vie du soldat, telle était la mienne à laquelle je n'ai jamais pu m'habituer entièrement. Et poutant cetten vie factice, contraire à la loi naturelle, n'est pas dépourvue d'une certaine douceur, compensation de la perte de la liberté. Les événements heureux semblent directement envoyés par la Providence ; les

moments difficiles se supportent d'autant plus patiemment qu'on n'est pas la cause des circonstances qui les ont produits ; on n'a pas comme dans la vie commune à se reprocher d'avoir mal jugé, d'avoir fait de faux calculs, d'avoir mal usé de son initiative.

Pierre-Irénée Jacob : Le Journal Inédit d'un pharmacien de la Grande Armée Bulletin de la Société D'Histoire de la Pharmacie (1966) Vol 18 p201

Translation:

…I made very serious reflections on this singular way of traveling with the army. One stopped being his own guide and his own arbiter, one somehow stopped being a man; to march or to stop, according to the will of an invisible power which directs you; such is the condition of the life of the soldier, such was mine, to which I have never been able to entirely get used to. Yet this fictitious life, contrary to the natural law, is not devoid of a certain sweetness that compensates for the loss of liberty. The happy events seem sent directly by Providence; the difficult moments are endured all the more patiently because they are caused by circumstances; it is not like in the common life where one blames oneself for having judged wrongly, for having made false calculations or for having misused one's initiative.

Appendix
Daily Telegraph Articles
Written in Balad, Iraq, in 2005

10 Jan, 2005
Arrival

The first week of my deployment to the Middle East started badly. I was impressed by the bleak landscape which was vivid white to the horizon. It appeared barren except for a few clumps of conifers but no grass or undergrowth. There were people scattered everywhere I could see, all dressed in varying colours and styles. I looked down the mountain and into the valley and thought that if I were to be injured on this deployment that this would be the place. I was in Vail, Colorado at a Conference for Orthopaedic Surgeons in the US Military and sure enough, I injured my ankle on the first day of skiing. This left me three weeks to get back to operational fitness which I managed without much time to spare.

I reported for the first stage of the deployment to an ADF staging facility in a country in the Persian Gulf where I met the other members of the deploying medical team. We were busy for twenty-four hours to add to our kitting, training and briefing. We were then sent on the last leg of our journey, carried on a RAAF Hercules, wearing our body armour and helmet and carrying our rifles. All had gone smoothly. Military travel has a few quirks. For example, if you arrive one minute before reporting time, departure will be one hour behind schedule. However, if you arrive one minute after reporting time, departure would have been on schedule to the second. Reporting time and departure time are given well in advance but are always changed, invariably the reporting time being brought forwards and the departure time being put backwards.

Reaching our destination, it was immediately apparent that this is a much bigger military operation than I have ever experienced before. Everything is huge, the size of the base, the numbers of soldiers and airmen, the heavy equipment, the vehicles, the constant flights of aircraft and helicopters. The organisation and logistics involved must be on a massive scale.

The departing ADF medical team met us as soon as we got off the aircraft. I know most of them but they are difficult to recognise in body armour, helmets and goggles. We were next greeted by our new colleagues from the Senior Coalition Partner. We will be working with them for the next few months and they gave us a warm welcome and were very complimentary about the departing Australian team, indicating that we have big boots to fill.

The surroundings were an immediate impact and became more apparent as we were driven to our living and working area. The first impression was of constant noise and activity occurring in bare dirt which sets up a steady flow of dust in the air. This gives everything a tinge of the same reddish-tan colour as it settles. We looked out at flat land, varieties of buildings, concrete blocks, sandbags and Humvees. Ironically, we also see Australian eucalyptus trees.

I do not expect to set foot off base for the entire time that I am here.

The accommodation is luxurious compared to previous deployments. I was shown to a demountable hut with a large room to myself and a shared toilet and en-suite with a HOT shower! The Senior Coalition Partner calls it a trailer even though it has no wheels, no tow-bar connection and no number-plate.

The weather is dry and mild during the day and cool but comfortable at night.

The next steps are to look at the medical facility where I will be working and then a better look around the base.

18 Feb, 2005
ADF Med. Det. Balad

The base is a little patch of the USA in Iraq and we are a little bit of Australia within that base. We are 20 health professionals deployed with the ADF Med. Det. Balad and there are also six RAAF Air Traffic Controllers.

We spend our workday with our colleagues from the Senior Coalition Partner but we see other team members during the day and also socialise off duty.

The Senior Coalition Partner has made us very welcome and there is great interest and affection for all things Australian, including our accents. However, our team values our time with each other when we create an illusion of being at home.

We see each other at meals and around our accommodation and exchange rumours and undisputed facts in the tradition of the Furphy of World War 1. A spare room in one of the huts has been converted into the Wombat Bar where we drink soft drinks and wish they were something better. Familiar icons are scattered about so that it seems like a home rather than a dusty base in Iraq which we cannot leave for months. Comforters include long out of date magazines and newspapers, familiar sweets and biscuits and our own TV which is tuned to the multi-channel US Air Force service. There is a small backyard of pebbles fenced by sandbags and the wall of the hut and is covered with camouflage netting.

I am with the broad mix that is typical on an ADF deployment and with the customary desire to help one another succeed during our time together. The officer-in-command and the Senior NCO always set the tone of these deployments and we have been blessed with our leadership on this unique and demanding deployment. We have Reservist and full-time Navy, Army and Air Force members. There are Medical Officers, Nursing Officers and Medics. Some like me are deployed for three months but the majority is here for six months and many have left young families at home. The separation can be hard going but our team is cheerful, proud of its achievements while representing the ADF and Australia and pleased to be contributing to the improvement of a country that is distressed.

We have some typical characters who keep us amused despite trials such as unwelcome ordnance regularly arriving on the scene unannounced. One was a rocket which landed in the front yard of the hospital and obligingly did not explode but still left a two-metre crater on impact. It took the explosive disposal gentlemen three attempts to get rid of it with a 'controlled explosion' which wobbled the tents and shook out the dust.

Travel off the base is banned because of the dangers and many areas inside the base are also off limits because of secrecy or threat of insurgent action. House arrest must be like this.

We see the air traffic controllers intermittently in the mess, workplace or accommodation. They have a regular Sunday afternoon BBQ squeezed into a narrow walkway between sandbags. The sausages come from Germany, the potato chips from Kuwait and the imitation beer from the USA but it is good enough to seem like Sunday at home. We catch up on Australian news and sports results and make derogatory comparisons between American football and our favourite Australian code. This deployment has produced a healthy coalition of fans of Rugby Union, Rugby League and Australian Rules.

The Medical Team reciprocated last week with a BBQ beside the MWR (Morale, Welfare and Recreation) tent, which was memorable for our Squadron Leader Intensive Care Specialist showing signs of pyromania as she piled the wood on the fire and threatening to do more damage than all of the mortar bombs delivered by the insurgents.

Mon, 31 Jan, 2005
The Base

The base is huge but my everyday life revolves around my hut, the hospital, the mess, the gym, the cinema and the PX store. The closest is a five-minute walk from my hut and the closest mess is ten minutes away. The rest are a twenty-minute walk away. There is a bus service but more speed and convenience would be better and so I buy a second-hand bike for US$100. This allows a good look around the base.

I circuit the base on the perimeter road which takes about an hour. This provides a rare chance to look at the countryside outside but afterwards I am told that this is not a good place to ride as the insurgents are suspected of firing small arms into the base. Bullet holes in the bus that runs the perimeter road are cited as evidence. I now keep to the roads in the main area of the base.

Red-brown dust is everywhere. It floats in the air and settles so that the whole lot has the same red-brown shading. The scene looks like an old sepia photograph which has been lightly coloured.

The land is completely flat and there is no vegetation except for eucalypt trees. This was a major base during the Saddam regime and the old permanent infrastructure was visible and still being used. It was of poor construction and has not withstood heavy use over the past year. Buildings such as accommodation, cinema and dining halls are occupied but look like neglected warehouses. The roads have not survived the constant heavy traffic and the bitumen is cracking, there are pot-holes and the gutters are falling over. The footpaths have turned to dirt. Large concrete shelters are dotted around and look like upside down dishes. Many temporary buildings have been built. Sandbags protect all buildings up to mid-window level and there are modular concrete walls and bunkers everywhere. Any vacant land is full of heavy equipment, vehicles and containers of stores.

Everything appears random and chaotic.

The flow of vehicles is non-stop. The Humvee is the workhorse and comes in various shapes and configurations for different tasks. There are many heavy transporters. I counted 17 in one convoy each alternating with an armed Humvee.

There are many personnel walking, running and driving in degrees of readiness varying from wearing gym clothes to full body protection and armed.

Watchtowers and a circling Blackhawk helicopter secure the perimeter.

25 Jan, 2005
The Hospital

The hospital is a five-minute walk from my trailer along an untrustworthy path which is a mixture of concrete pavers, clay, dust and pebbles. It is the wet season and rain changes it to deep mud, lakes of water and slime which lies around for days. More often, the weather is mild, clear and pleasant. Tonnes of pebbles are everywhere to protect against the mud and keep boots cleaner but will become projectiles when a mortar bomb or rocket lands.

The hospital is a giant version of the RAAF's Air Transportable Hospital with a backbone of a 150m long corridor and many components extending out like ribs. The operating theatres (or "ORs" as the Senior Coalition Partner calls them) are basically shipping containers which become room size when unfolded. There are three ORs and ominously each has an extra operating table stacked against the wall so that two operations can be performed in each OR during the frequent mass casualties. They have low ceilings, the equipment is squeezed in and staff are cramped for room, like our deployable ADF ORs.

Everything is like 'our' deployable hospitals but much bigger. It is under rows of tents erected end to end. The beds are litters on collapsible legs. All equipment and fittings are made for transport and rugged use and are functional rather than luxurious.

Australians are essential personnel for the two wards of the intensive care unit which is large and over-stretched. One of my enduring memories from this deployment will be noise everywhere and ICU is a generous contributor. There is no piped suction apparatus and so each patient on a ventilator has portable suction as noisy as a jackhammer.

I am introduced to my patients and it is apparent how different it will be from my Sydney practice. One is an Iraqi civilian who suffered terrible injuries from a bomb, which is an IED (Improvised Explosive Device) in army-speak. His relatives took him from a local hospital and dropped him at the front gate of the base. The bomb sprayed him with high-speed pebbles causing a combination of blast injuries and multiple penetrating injuries. He has had brain surgery by the neurosurgeon, an eye removed by the eye surgeon, insertion of chest drains and abdominal surgery by the general surgeons and a tracheostomy by the ear, nose and throat surgeon. My orthopaedic colleagues have amputated his left leg below the knee and we are trying to save his broken left arm which has lost most of its skin. His broken right leg is in an external fixator. He is desperately ill from his injuries and infection.

Within days, we amputate his left leg above the knee and later through the hip. His left arm is amputated through the shoulder. Response to treatment is slow but he is eventually transferred for his protracted recovery.

I learn that multiple injuries treated by multiple specialists happen frequently.

19 Feb, 2005
A Typical Day

My alarm goes at 0500 and I immediately get out of bed and turn on the heater because the nights and mornings are very cold. Often, I jump back into bed for a short time but I have always shaved, showered and walked to the mess for breakfast by 0600.

I will be in the hospital by 0700 to check the sicker patients and possibly join the main ward round.

The routine theatre list starts every day at 0730. The list today was typical.

Firstly, there was a man who had lost a leg through the hip following a bomb blast about four days previously. The stump had been left open and so was cleaned and partly sutured and partly skin grafted.

The second was a patient with a fractured foot and ankle which needed opening and fixing with a plate and screws.

Next was a patient with a fracture of the lower leg and severe loss of skin and muscle following a bomb blast. The bone was held with an external fixation frame but there was still a large hole in his soft tissues. The wound was washed and re-dressed for later closure.

Meanwhile, the urgent new admissions start to arrive. The first has been showered with shrapnel from the explosion of a car driven by a suicide bomber. One thigh has been penetrated by a fragment which has damaged the main artery. This is repaired by the vascular surgeon. Another fragment has passed completely through his upper arm, fracturing his bone on its journey. I enlarge the entrance and exit wounds so that they can be washed and cleaned and then hold the fracture with pins through both fragments of bone joined by a frame.

Another patient has arrived before we have finished. He is another blast victim with a fractured hand and divided tendons and a fracture of his leg. The hand is washed and pinned with a wire for later repair of the tendon. The leg is held with external fixation pins and frame.

All of these patients are Iraqi citizens.

I have lunch in the hospital mess when there is time or meals are brought to the operating suite in plastic containers. I get to the main mess if it is a quiet day.

We see outpatients in the physiotherapy clinic in the afternoon. These may be coalition forces with similar problems to those I usually see in my practice at home such as knee, shoulder and ankle injuries following sport or work injuries. Others are Iraqis who are still recovering from severe blast and gunshot injuries. Some have been in fixation frames for months but the bones are healing slowly because of the severity of the injury. Some have a long-term disabling nerve, muscle and tendon injuries. We see amputees in wheelchairs. I am unsure whether there is a limb fitting service in Iraq.

We have a morbidity and mortality meeting once a week when we learn some hard truths about our performance.

Dinner is at 1800 at the mess.

The ADF Medical Detachment meets once a week at 1900 for a briefing from the officer-in-command and to reassure ourselves that we are much better than the Americans. We revise our weapon training with rifles and pistols.

Evenings are usually for relaxing though I am on call one night in three.

Some afternoons I get the chance to go to the gym or ride my bike.

No alcoholic drinks are allowed on this deployment out of respect for our presence in a Muslim country. I enjoy wine, whiskey and beer but can live quite happily without. I have been on deployments when restricted alcohol has been permitted but my opinion is that a total ban works much better.

The medical team is composed of men and women and any form of relationship developing between members while on deployment is strictly forbidden. I have never been aware of a commanding officer needing to enforce this order and I attribute this to the self-discipline and quality of ADF personnel.

5 Feb, 2005
Mascal

The daily workload fluctuates and my busiest day started at 7:30 am while changing for a routine list in the operating theatre. A nearby large explosion shook the tent and threw dust off the ceiling. We could see a large cloud of dust and smoke and people running towards the gate of the base but then the 'Red Alert' siren sounded. We put on our armour and helmets and huddled in the operating theatre which was protected by sandbags.

Many Iraqi citizens had been injured when a suicide car bomber had driven to the gate and detonated. The rapid influx of patients stretched resources almost to breaking point.

My notes remind me of a few patients I helped treat. Most had multiple injuries

One had a shattered leg with a division of nerves, blood vessels and muscle. Immediate amputation was necessary. He also had a brain injury and eye perforation. There were multiple lacerations to his face and legs from shrapnel.

Another had similar severe damage to a leg which was amputated through the knee. He also had facial lacerations, a fracture of the jaw and perforation of his eye. His hands were lacerated and broken.

Shrapnel had penetrated the abdomen of another victim and his bowel was exposed and perforated.

Flying shrapnel causes injuries. A patient had lacerations and fractures to both legs and one bled severely from major arterial damage. This was controlled but we amputated a few days later. The blast of the explosion also causes injuries and this man had brain and chest damage.

Another victim had a perforation of bowel and tearing of the liver from the blast and lacerations and fractures to his face and hands from shrapnel.

Some were less severe. One man came in unconscious but recovered quickly. Several victims had bruising and minor lacerations that were swiftly treated.

Triage is the first step when many casualties arrive at once. A senior doctor sets the priorities for those needing the most urgent treatment and allocates resuscitation and theatre resources.

The second step is assessment and resuscitation in the emergency department by teams of specialist doctors, nurses and medics.

The third step is surgical treatment in the operating theatre by general surgeons, orthopaedic surgeons, neurosurgeons and eye surgeons supported by operating theatre and anaesthetic staff.

The fourth step is continuing care in the intensive care unit by specialist physicians and specialist nurses.

These teams functioned well on this occasion and all these patients survived.

30 Jan, 2005
Election Day

Sunday, 30 January 2005. Election Day in Iraq.

The work has been busy for the first five weeks of the deployment with surges after bombings and a steady flow the rest of the time. It has been quieter for the past week but the intelligence is that the insurgents are saving their ammunition for the big one today and mass casualties are expected.

The security level has been increased. All personnel must be available at instant notice and must wear armour and carry weapons. We must walk in small groups when out of the hospital but a large number gathering in one place can mean many casualties if bombed and so all recreational areas are closed and food from the mess is wrapped in foil and carried to our huts on plastic plates.

Yesterday was business as usual with two acute orthopaedic cases. Both were Iraqi soldiers with a gunshot wound to the knee. One wound was from a heavy machine gun and the round had caused so much damage to nerves, blood vessels, muscle and bone that amputation of the leg above the knee was necessary. The other was from a high-velocity rifle but the bullet had passed superficially and cleaning the wound was sufficient.

There was also work for the other specialities. Two patients had gunshot wounds to the head, one fatal, but the other the bullet had miraculously missed all vital structures. There were a few blast injuries causing eye and face injuries. A pregnant Iraqi woman in labour was brought to the front gate which is something different for a military hospital.

Today, I collect my breakfast of bacon, doughnut, pineapple and grapefruit. I put my magazine of ammunition in my pocket, my dog-tag around my neck, my armour over my body, my helmet and protective goggles on my head, sling my rifle over my shoulder and I set off on my day's work as an orthopaedic surgeon.

The day follows a familiar routine with ward round, administration and acute admissions. These arrive at the usual tempo and usual mixture of gunshot wounds, blast injuries and the odd industrial or motor vehicle injury for good measure.

Some of the day is spent watching Iraqi civilians queuing to vote on CNN television.

By the time I collect my dinner of stir-fried pork, rice and cabbage, it is apparent that the voting has occurred in relative safety and the casualties for all specialists have been far fewer than feared.

6 Feb, 2005
Noise

I have never been on a noisier deployment. It is like living on a busy main road next to an airport with a construction site on one side and loud neighbours on the other.

This is a major air base with all manner of aircraft coming and going. There are small cargo aircraft, giant cargo aircraft, military aircraft and chartered civilian aircraft. There are cargo, utility and combat helicopters. However, the fighters are the loudest, particularly as they fly in small groups, usually in the middle of the night. The raw power of their engines is inspiring, but it was bad for sleeping for the first few days until I adjusted.

The hospital helipad sits between the hospital and my hut. The Blackhawks land so close that the hut shakes. They arrive frequently, sometimes two or three at a time. Most of our patients are delivered by helicopter and so, at first, I feared the sound meant trouble but it became apparent that Blackhawks also deliver blood and other supplies and evacuate patients and so now, I hear them arrive without apprehension.

The activity and noise on the base never stop and is a loud background growl. I see people and vehicles about even when I am called to the hospital in the early hours of the morning. There is constant traffic noise from multitudes of Humvees, container transporters, buses, military trucks and semi-trailers, personnel carriers, tanks and any other sort of military vehicle that exists.

There are diesel generators everywhere. All power is generated on base and each unit has its own generators with backups. The hospital has a good selection close by and they can drown normal conversation, particularly when the smaller, hard-running backups are operating.

The base is being reconstructed after being knocked about during the war and the facilities are being expanded. Construction equipment and heavy earth moving equipment are operating non-stop.

The accommodation huts are close together and all have air conditioning units which run constantly, producing a constant loud buzz.

Even the interior of the hospital is noisy with air conditioning, suction equipment, water supply pumps, sterilisers, flapping tents, tradesmen's tools and sundry electrical equipment.

Humans are remarkably adaptable. On all my deployments, my first reaction to an unpleasant environment has been that I would not be able to adapt but within a few days, the noise becomes simply part of the background.

20 Feb, 2005
The World Outside

I enjoy traveling and have a healthy curiosity about foreign countries. I would like to get out and have a good look around Iraq and see the countryside and the way of life of the local citizens. However, I will be confined on base for the duration of the deployment which is probably just as well considering the dangers.

I have some limited opportunities to look through the wire at the world outside.

I have ridden my bike around the perimeter road. I could see flat land, scrub-like vegetation, and dead-looking reeds. There were small patches of grass and larger areas of cultivation. I saw a tractor towing a plough through a paddock and the driver waved. I saw a woman in a colourful shawl leading some black cows in the company of her brightly clothed children. The children became excited at the sight of me and jumped up and down and yelled, a miniature and distant version of the laughing children who swarmed over us in East Timor.

We can climb onto the roof of a building in the hospital yard and look over the concrete block wall to the perimeter wire and watchtower and beyond.

There is a concrete ditch running adjacent to the wire fence and this is presumably a storm water drain though it is hard to imagine it ever filling. There are sand dunes on the edge of the ditch with stunted grass and weeds. The appearance reminds me of the entrance of the Torrens River to West Beach in my old home town of Adelaide.

Beyond is flat countryside with a mixture of bare red clay, dead reeds, scattered low palms, and one small area of green grass. This vista is viewed through a constant haze of red dust and stretches out to the horizon.

I can see the horizon better with binoculars. There appear to be larger trees further away and there is a small clump of quite large palm trees. I can see a flat-roofed double-storied farmhouse and large farm buildings. There must be a road to the house as there is a row of telegraph poles and a power line.

Further around there is a village on the horizon. There is a tall large water tower. There are several freestanding flat-roofed tan houses, which are in the style I would expect in the Middle East. There also appears to be a row of modern town houses joined together with gabled roofs. There is a mosque with a light green dome. There appears to be an industrial area or a power station.

That is all that I will see of the outside world for three months.

After the massacre. Children without parents or relatives in Mother Teresa's orphanage in Kigali, Rwanda

Kigali market, Rwanda

Letter from an Australian girl addressed to 'Children of Rwanda'

Drawing by the boy who lost both legs below the knee (see Introduction). He said that he drew himself as the figure on the right of the picture with artificial legs

Rwandan Patriotic Army barracks viewed from the UN hospital

Street scene while on truck run in Kigali, Rwanda

UN hospital in Kigali, Rwanda, damaged during massacre and later civil war

Australian Army field hospital in Vanimo, PNG, treating tsunami survivors

After surgery in tent operating theatre in Vanimo, PNG

Gifted a souvenir in Vanimo, PNG. The shopkeeper refused payment

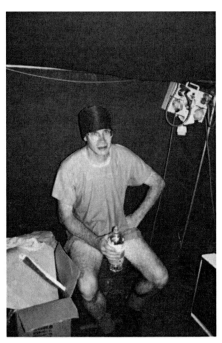

The author hot, exhausted and soaked in sweat after operating in the tent, Vanimo, PNG

The author with the owner of the airstrip in Bougainville

The hospital and accommodation under shelter in Loloho, Bougainville

Ambulances burnt and destroyed during the civil war, Bougainville

Selling petrol and diesel in Dili, East Timor

Visiting the South Korean army in East Timor

Message from the UN Commander, East Timor

The wet season in Dili, East Timor. The Environmental Health Team usually choose somewhere healthy and dry

Japanese acknowledgement of battlefield on Guadalcanal, the Solomon Islands

Local interest in RAAF Caribou landed on a grass strip in a remote island, the Solomon Islands

The USAF hospital in Balad, Iraq. (US Defence Dept photo)

A Blackhawk helicopter delivering a casualty in Balad, Iraq. (US Defence Dept photo)

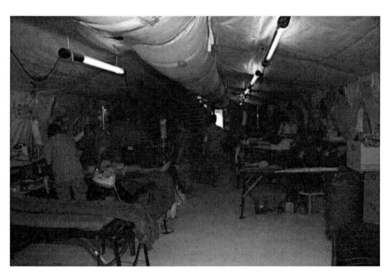
Ward in USAF hospital Balad, Iraq

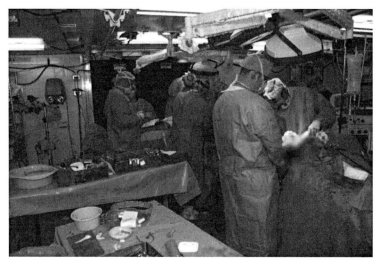

Operating theatre in USAF hospital Balad, Iraq. Note two operations occurring simultaneously during mass casualty

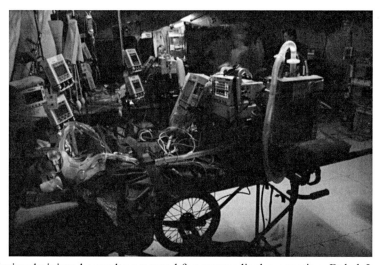

Seriously injured casualty prepared for aeromedical evacuation. Balad, Iraq

Accommodation in Balad, Iraq

Iraqi Air Force MIGs destroyed before leaving ground. Balad, Iraq

Destroyed and burnt out trucks and fuel tankers. Balad, Iraq

Two rows of container accommodation joined by overhead shelter in Tarin Kowt, Afghanistan

Receiving a casualty in Tarin Kowt, Afghanistan. (Netherlands Defence Force photo)

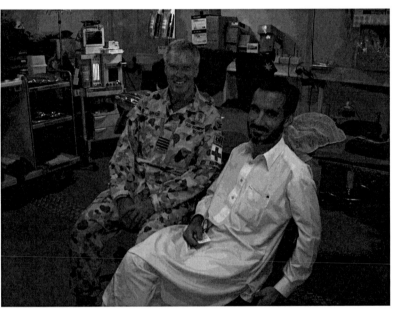
Sitting in the operating theatre when visited by the local surgeon.
Tarin Kowt, Afghanistan

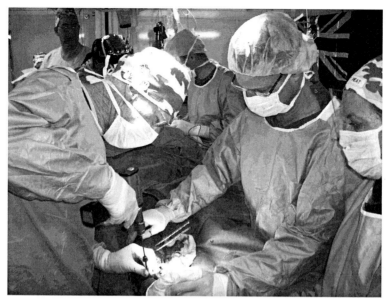

Application of an external fixation frame to a fractured leg. A very frequent operation for a military orthopaedic surgeon. Tarin Kowt, Afghanistan

Receiving a local Afghan casualty. Tarin Kowt, Afghanistan

Further Reading

Kevin O'Halloran, *Pure Massacre,* Big Sky Publishing

Nessen, Lounsbury, Hetz, *War Surgery in Afghanistan and Iraq*, Borden Institute

Owens, Belmont, *Combat Orthopaedic Surgery*, Stryker

Peter Cosgrove, *My Story*, Harper Collins

Ashley Mallett, *The Diggers' Doctor*, Wakefield Press

Chris Coppola, *Made a Difference for That One,* iUniverse

Stephen Tanner, *Afghanistan*, Da Capo Press

David Kilcullen, *The Accidental Guerrilla*, Scribe

Sharon Bown, *One Woman's War and Peace*, Exisle

Louise Richardson, *What Terrorists Want,* John Murray

Alistair Horne, *A Savage War of Peace*, NYRB

Jim Molan, *Running the War in Iraq*, Harper Collins

W Deane-Butcher, *Fighter Squadron Doctor,* Self-published

E P F Lynch Edited by Will Davies, *Somme Mud,* Penguin

Steve Coll, *Directorate S,* Penguin

Glossary of Terms/Abbreviations

Use of capital letters and abbreviations loosely conform to the instructions in:

Australian Defence Force Publication ADFP 102
Defence Force Writing Standards

Capital first letters are used for the following:
Ranks e.g. Commander, Lieutenant-Colonel, Wing Commander
Category e.g. Medical Officer, Nursing Officer
Appointment e.g. Commanding Officer
ADF Services i.e. Navy, Army, Air Force
(Lower case first letters are used for services from other countries or if used in general terms i.e. navy, army, air force.)

Abbreviations, medical jargon and military jargon appearing in the book are listed below:

AASM	Australian Active Service Medal
ADF	Australian Defence Force
AFP	Australian Federal Police
AK47	High velocity military rifle (Russian)
AME	Aero-Medical Evacuation
APC	Armoured Personnel Carrier
AQIS	Australian Quarantine and Inspection Service
ASM	Australian Service Medal
ASLAV	Australian Light Armoured Vehicle
C-130	Hercules transport aircraft
CDF	Chief of Defence Force
CHK	Central Hospital Kigali
CO	Commanding Officer
DG	Dangerous Goods
Dossing down	Rough sleeping conditions
FTS	Full Time Service
HMMWV	High Mobility Multipurpose Wheeled Vehicle
Hoochie	Plastic sheet for minimal shelter at night
Huey	UH1 Iroquois helicopter
Humvee	HMMWV (see above)
HVGSW	High velocity gunshot wound
ICRC	International Committee of the Red Cross/Crescent
IED	Improvised Explosive Device

INTERFET	International Force in East Timor
Loadmaster	RAAF NCO responsible for passengers and cargo on RAAF aircraft
MEAO	Middle East Area of Operation
Mess	Military dining room. Capital letters for a specific mess, i.e. Officers Mess, Sergeants Mess. Lower case letter for non-specific mess.
MO	Medical Officer
MRE	Meal Ready to Eat
MSF	Médicins sans Frontières
NATO	North Atlantic Treaty Organisation
NCO	Non-Commissioned Officer (e.g. Sergeant)
NGO	Non-Government Organisation
NO	Nursing Officer
PMG	Peace Monitoring Group
PNG	Papua New Guinea
RAAF	Royal Australian Air Force
RAF	Royal Air Force
RAMSI	Regional Assistance Mission to the Solomon Islands
Rat Packs	Ration Packs or MREs
RPA	Rwandan Patriotic Army
RPG	Rocket Propelled Grenade
RTA	Return to Australia
SAM	Surface to Air Missile
SOMOS	Society of Military Orthopaedic Surgeons
SF	Special Forces. Highly trained combat soldiers (e.g. Commandos, SAS)
SQN	Squadron
UAV	Unmanned Aerial Vehicle
UD	Unauthorised Discharge (of weapon e.g. rifle)
UN	United Nations
UNAMIR	United Nations Assistance Mission for Rwanda
UNTAET	United Nations Transitional Administration in East Timor
USAF	United States Air Force